MW01480171

The way to Nirvana; six lectures on ancient Buddhism as a discipline of salvation

Louis de La Vallée Poussin

THE WAY TO NIRVĀṆA

SIX LECTURES ON ANCIENT BUDDHISM AS A DISCIPLINE OF SALVATION

HIBBERT LECTURES, MANCHESTER COLLEGE, OXFORD, FEBRUARY—APRIL 1916

by

L. DE LA VALLÉE POUSSIN
professeur à l'Université de Gand

Cambridge:
at the University Press
1917

À MES COLLÈGUES

PAUL FREDERICQ ET HENRI PIRENNE

EN TÉMOIGNAGE

DE RESPECT ET D'AFFECTION

PRÉFACE

JE suis fort heureux d'avoir accepté l'invitation des Hibbert Trustees et de mon excellent ami le Dr J. E. Carpenter. C'était une bonne occasion de faire une sorte d'examen de conscience et d'exposer brièvement et clairement ce que je pense d'un des aspects du Bouddhisme, le vieux Bouddhisme monastique et ses théories sur le salut. Même ainsi circonscrit, le sujet reste vaste, et sur combien de points on pourrait épiloguer à perte de vue ! C'est un des *drawbacks* du genre *Lectures* qu'il faut sacrifier les nuances ; mais c'est un de ses avantages qu'il faut aller à l'essentiel. À sacrifier quelques bouquets d'arbres et une bonne partie de la frondaison, on obtient une meilleure idée de la forêt. Et couper, parfois avec un peu d'arbitraire, des avenues dans la forêt, c'est, tout compte fait, le seul moyen de la parcourir. Les sentiers sont charmants, mais ils égarent.

Jamais je ne me serais hasardé à parler en anglais si je n'avais pu compter, et sur l'extrême bienveillance des maîtres et des étudiants de Manchester College,—bienveillance qui prêta tant de charme à une familière et exquise hospitalité,

—et sur le concours de mes amis de Cambridge. Tous, anciens et nouveaux, rivalisèrent de zèle. Il fallait expulser solécismes et barbarismes de ma phrase anglaise; il fallait, tâche plus difficile et particulièrement ingrate, m'apprendre à prononcer d'une manière à peu près intelligible et les mots et les périodes. Dans ce double effort, Miss C. M. Ridding a déployé une patience et une ingéniosité admirables. Je garde aussi un souvenir ému de la bonté avec laquelle le Master d'Emmanuel et Mrs P. Giles ont, pendant les vacances de Noël 1915 et la veille de chacune de mes expériences oratoires en février et mars 1916, écouté mes élucubrations bouddhiques, rectifiant l'accent, donnant leurs soins à la couleur des voyelles et aux aspirations,—si nécessaires et si difficiles,—proposant des variantes favorables à l'élocution. À ces exercices, le texte ne manquait pas de s'améliorer, pensée et style. Il doit aussi beaucoup à M. E. J. Rapson, professeur de sanscrit à l'Université de Cambridge, qui a lu très utilement les épreuves, et à M. E. J. Thomas qui a laissé sa marque sur toutes les pages du manuscrit.

L. V. P.

16 *Décembre* 1916

CONTENTS

CHAP. PAGE

I. ORIGINS OF THE INDIAN DISCIPLINES OF SALVATION 1

I. Religions and disciplines of salvation, p. 1. II. Old Aryan beliefs, the dead, gods, sacrifice, p. 10. III. Brahman speculation, theology, ritualism, 're-death,' *ātman*, p. 16.

II. THE BUDDHIST SOUL 30

I. Buddhism a form of rationalism, p. 30. II. Buddhist psychology; contradictions, p. 34. III. There is no Self: Man is a chariot, p. 35. IV. There is reward of actions in a future life, p. 45. V. Whether Buddhists deny rebirth or migration of a soul, while maintaining migration of *karman* or character, p. 47. VI. Buddhists admit a sort of soul, p. 50.

III. BUDDHIST DEFINITION OF KARMAN . . 57

I. Introductory, p. 57. II. Ancient history of Karman, p. 60. III. Karman is volition and voluntary action, p. 67. IV. Karman is moral action, p. 73.

IV. THE DOCTRINE OF KARMAN AND TRANSMIGRATION, COSMOGONY, THEOGONY . 80

I. Mechanism of transmigration, p. 80. II. Classification of actions and mechanism of their fructification, p. 88. III. Destiny, free-will, solidarity, p. 94. IV. Cosmogony, p. 100. V. Theogony, p. 101.

CHAP. PAGE

V. Nirvāṇa 107

I. Introductory. Pessimism and deliverance or Nirvāṇa. Difficulties in ascertaining the nature of deliverance, p. 107. II. Etymology and meaning of the word Nirvāṇa. Three opinions on the state of a Saint after death, p. 113. III. Annihilation, p. 116. IV. 'Unqualified deliverance,' p. 123. V. Conclusion. Scholastic views on the conflicting statements in the Scriptures, p. 132.

VI. The Path to Nirvāṇa 139

I. The Path is the eradication of desire, p. 139. II. A middle way between asceticism and indulgence, p. 142. III. A threefold training in the Buddhist truths, p. 151. IV. A skilful practice of trances, p. 159. V. Conclusion, p 166.

Index 169

CHAPTER I

INDIAN DISCIPLINES OF SALVATION

I. Religions and disciplines of salvation. II. Old Aryan beliefs, the dead, gods, sacrifice. III. Brahman speculation, theology, ritualism, 're-death,' *ātman.*

I

General definitions are always somewhat misleading and give rise to discussion. But some definition of the title of these lectures is necessary. 'Buddhism as a discipline of salvation' is to be contrasted with 'Buddhism as a religion.'

There are and there have been in India, since the beginning, a number of religions, religions properly so called. They present an endless variety; they often differ essentially one from another; they belong to distinct types of civilisation. But, although some are polytheistic, some monotheistic, and a larger number tinged with pantheism; although some are pagan, dishonest, superstitious and magical, and some lofty and pure in every respect, some logical and cold, and some mystical and passionate,—all of them nevertheless come under the concept of religion as this word is generally understood by modern students of religious history. Whatever be their diversity, all were 'made' to meet, and they do meet in some manner, the needs of Man living in society, needs supernatural, moral and secular, needs individual and social. They teach a superhuman power, whatever be the nature and the dignity of this power; they explain the duties of Man towards it, or, more uncompromisingly, the right *modus vivendi* of Man with it; they have prayers or formulas, sacrifices, sacraments. They are concerned with the welfare of the dead, and also with personal welfare in this life; they have devices and ceremonies for the work and the anxieties of everyday life, for illnesses and for sins, which are often another kind of illness. They teach a general rule of conduct, and penetrate the Law of family or of tribe, for there is no clear and constant distinction between profane and sacred things.

Although the religions of India are usually quite Indian, quite Hindu, parallels are to be found to each of them outside India. Hindu is the word we use to emphasize the special and composite character of the Indian civilisation.

There is no Sanskrit word which covers the

whole field of beliefs and practices that the word 'religion' suggests. But if we examine the many words which convey a religious meaning, *yajña*, 'sacrifice,' magical to some extent, *pūjā*, 'worship,' often idolatrous, *bhakti*, 'devotion,' *dharma*, moral and social rule, 'law' and virtue, we see that, while Indian 'sacrifice,' 'cult,' 'devotion,' 'law,' are quite Hindu, and are unlike the Semitic sacrifice, the Egyptian cults, the Christian love of God, the Roman *jus majorum*, they are nevertheless simply human (*humain tout court*) as far as their leading motive and their 'philosophy' are concerned.

For instance, the gods and the rites of the Vedic religion are quite Hindu; they differ largely from the Iranian types, not to mention the other religions of the Ancient World. Nevertheless Vedism is clearly a branch of the Indo-European tradition; it is akin to all naturalistic and patriarchal beliefs the world over, while it is contaminated to a no small extent with the common fancies of the old and always living paganism.

Side by side with the religions properly so called, there arose in India from about the seventh century B.C.—to last for many centuries, attracting thousands of adherents and exercising a strong influence on the Indian religions—a number of 'disciplines' with a special character of their own.

They cannot be exactly described either as philosophies or as religions. We have to see what name is the right name for them.

They are 'disciplines,' that is bodies of doctrines and practices, together with a rule of life, aiming at a practical end,—the Indian word is *mārga*, 'path,' or *yāna*, 'vehicle,'—and, from this point of view, they are something more than philosophies, theories, or scholasticisms. But it is doubtful whether they can be styled 'religions.'

In contrast with religions, the disciplines are made for ascetics, for ascetics only. Further they are purely personal or individualistic, that is they do not care for one's neighbour or for the dead. They are unsocial and often antisocial: they deprecate and often prohibit marriage. As a rule, they originate sects or orders and it may be churches, but such social formations are not essential to them: even in Buddhism, where the Master and the Church are all important, a belief exists that, in the days to come, when the Master is forgotten, the Church dissolved and Buddhism extinct, there will arise, from time to time, 'individual saints' (*pratyekabuddha*) who will be, by themselves, perfect Buddhists, living alone in the wilderness, like a rhinoceros, without companions or pupils.

Another feature of the disciplines is that they are not concerned with mundane ends at all. The Buddhist teaching is clear to this effect: any action which aims at any advantage whatever in the present life, is bad.

These two characters may be found in some institutions of the West. There are, for instance, Christian sects or orders which are practically unconcerned with social and mundane interests; —and so far the Indian Paths could be described as 'individualist transcendent religions.' But they present a third character, in respect of which all non-Indian parallels prove inadequate, except the Sūfis, the best instance of a sect of Indian spirit outside India—a third character, in respect of which our western nomenclature is deficient.

Either the Indian ascetic does not believe in God; or, when he believes in God, he says, as the outspoken Sūfi or as Spinoza: "There is nothing but God. I am God." But the attitude of the Indian ascetic is not the attitude of the western philosopher, a Lucretius or a modern monist. For he has beliefs of his own, foreign to his occidental brothers. To put it shortly, he believes in transmigration and transmigration he dreads. His positivist or monist philosophy is therefore combined with a discipline, a Path, for he has to save himself, to liberate himself from transmigration.

Man migrates from existence to existence, driven by the wind of his actions: there must be a Path to deliverance from rebirth and death. This Path must be a certain knowledge or esoteric wisdom, or a certain sacrifice, or a certain asceticism, or a certain ecstatic meditation.

It is difficult to state accurately the position of prayer or worship and of morality in the disciplines.

Prayer or worship is never an essential part of the path. But it happens that an ascetic—for instance the Buddhist of the Mahāyāna school—believes that gods or divinised saints may help him towards the path, or even in climbing along the first slopes of the path: prayer and worship are, in such a case, useful or even necessary, but they have to be given up once the ascetic has somewhat advanced.

As concerns morality, no discipline admits that an immoral man can reach the path: a purgative process is deemed necessary[1]. But all disciplines are fond of stating that a saint is beyond merit and demerit, good deed and sin: no merit can accrue to him; no sin can soil him. In Mahāyāna Buddhism, active morality, gifts, self-sacrifice for the welfare of one's neighbour, are an essential part of the path. A saint is by definition

[1] "As a clean cloth free from stain duly takes the dye, so in Yasa, the noble youth, arose a pure, unstained insight into the doctrine."

a 'giver,' a 'compassionate': but his gifts are to be 'perfumed' with the knowledge of the transcendent truth that in reality there is no giver, no gift, no receiver (see below p. 78)[1].

By this Path, through this Ford (*tīrtha*), the ascetic will cross the ocean of transmigration, as well as the worlds of the gods or paradises. The ascetic believes in such worlds—for he is not a sceptic, he willingly admits the whole of the traditional or popular mythology—but he despises them; he despises, as a philosopher would say, every 'contingent' existence; he aims at something that is beyond the worlds, that is 'hypercosmical' (to translate the Buddhist idiom, *lokottara*), a mysterious somewhere, a somewhere that is eternal and 'free from sorrow,' and which is called sometimes 'deliverance' (*mokṣa*, *mukti*, *apavarga*), sometimes 'happiness' (*nirvṛti*, *naiḥśreyasa*), sometimes Nirvāṇa, that is 'refreshment' or 'peace.'

Such are the common features of these thoroughly Hindu institutions. In many respects, they are widely different one from another. Some are monist, pantheist or mystical (Upaniṣads, Vedānta, Yoga); some purposely atheist and rationalist (Jainism, Buddhism, Sāṃkhya). But

[1] An *exposé* of this intricate doctrine may be found in Hastings, *E.R.E.*, see 'Bodhisattva,' 'Mahāyāna,' 'Nihilism.'

they are sisters born from the same parents, namely disgust with life and love of mystery. If they do not agree concerning deliverance and the path to deliverance, they all pursue deliverance. The right name for them seems to be 'disciplines of salvation' or 'paths to deliverance[1].'

The time of Śākyamuni was an epoch of spiritual effervescence. Brahmans taught new doctrines. There were discussions and ideological tournaments. Scores of ascetics claimed to be discoverers of the Path, literally 'fordmakers,' who had found a ford across transmigration, or they claimed to be *buddhas*, that is 'awakened,' 'enlightened.' There was a large following for the leaders: people complained that, by their lessons and their example, "they caused the fathers to beget no sons, the wives to become widows and the families to die out." So large was the number of the candidates for deliverance: noblemen, merchants and treasurers, the *jeunesse dorée*, priests and men of priestly parentage, women, girls and wives and widows of good family, members of low caste or outcasts, Cāpā,

[1] On the notion of deliverance, see Mrs Rhys Davids' article 'Mokṣa,' in Hastings, *E.R.E.* VIII, pp. 770–774.

the daughter of a deer-stalker, Puṇṇā and Puṇṇikā, slave girls. And there was no resistance to whatever the supreme interest of deliverance could demand. Some—especially the Brahmans—preferred a solitary life in the forest; some formed groups of wandering mendicants. All abandoned the most sacred traditions, sacrifices, and the cult of the dead. All accepted the most stringent rule of life. To quote an extreme case, the disciple of the Jina practises a strict abstinence, and fears even to disturb the vermin; he objects to hot water and to hot meals, because the caldron harms the spirit of fire: such is his respect for life; he destroys his sins by extraordinary penances; finally, he starves himself to obtain salvation. Nothing can be too hard in the Path, if only the Path leads to the end.

This time was an epoch of exaltation, of serious and sagacious exaltation.

We know the story of two noble and fervent young men, Śāriputra, the future philosopher of Buddhism, and Maudgalyāyana, the future thaumaturge[1]. They had given their word to each other: "He who first discovers the Path to immortality shall tell the other." Their good

[1] See Rhys Davids' article on 'Moggallāna,' Hastings, *E.R.E.* VIII, p. 769.

luck led them to the great man for whom the common name or adjective, *buddha*, enlightened, has become a proper name, to Śākyamuni, the originator of the most celebrated among the Indian Paths of salvation.

We shall follow in their steps and respectfully hear the doctrine to which they clung. If, with the best will in the world, we cannot accept this doctrine, it is none the less worth considering.

But before becoming the disciples of Śākyamuni, it is necessary to study the origin of the ideas on which Buddhism—as well as the other disciplines of salvation—is built; and this inquiry will be our task for the present.

II

The disciplines of salvation arose from about the eighth to the sixth century B.C., in the middle and upper valley of the Ganges. At this time and in this place, there had been already a long and intimate intercourse between the two elements of the Hindu population.

On the one hand, were the aborigines, concerning whom we lack any direct information. It has been usual to assume that all the elements of the later Hindu civilisation which are not Āryan, or do not look Āryan, are due to their influence.

However this may be, modern inquiry as to the non-hinduized populations of India has been fruitful. For instance we know that the aborigines, as is the case with many savages, believed in reincarnations; they explained conception by the descent of some disincarnated spirit who had previously inhabited a human or an animal body or even a tree.

On the other hand, the Āryas, the Indo-European invaders of India, who, after settling in North West India, had in time reached the valley of the Ganges, bringing with them their language—which had already split up into dialects—their Book or Bible, the Veda, and their own civilisation, which was every day modified owing to an evolution due to manifold factors.

We are to study some aspects of this evolution, taking as our starting point the Āryan beliefs.

The Ārya is a member of a strongly organized body, the family of men in close relations with the gods, especially with the eternal domestic fire, and with the dead.

The whole fabric of domestic and social life is built on the beliefs concerning the dead. The destiny of the dead depends strictly on the services rendered to them by their descendants in the male line, born in legitimate wedlock and properly initiated into the religious rites of the family. Hence a strict obligation to marry, not only to ensure a man's personal happiness after death, but also that of his ancestors. Hence too a strict obligation to pass through a series of ceremonies of a sacramental character which affect the whole of a man's life from conception to initiation—with a period of study in the house of a preceptor—from marriage to death. No one is entitled to fulfil the funeral rites, the fortnightly banquets and the daily offerings for the dead, if he is not a member of the religious body. No one can hope for happiness after death if the rites are not properly performed for him at his death and in the ages to come by a member of this body.

Such were the conditions of welfare after death according to the oldest ideas of our race.

Superstitions connected with the belief that the dead are living in the grave, depending for this shadowy life on the offering poured on the grave, are not abolished in the Vedic civilisation. The general view is nevertheless an altogether hopeful one. The dead, who are called the Fathers, do not envy the living as did Achilles.

Some of them are now gods. The first of the mortals, Yama, "who first went over the great mountains and spied out a path for many, who found us a way of which we shall not be frustrated," Yama the King sits under a tree with Varuṇa the righteous god. The Fathers are gathered around him, drinking nectar, enjoying the libations of the living, enjoying also—and this point is worthy of notice—their own pious works, their sacrifices and their gifts, especially their gifts to the priests[1].

The abode of the Fathers is an immortal, unending world: "There make me immortal," says the Vedic poet, "where exist delight, joy, rejoicing, and joyance, where wishes are obtained." It is not a spiritual paradise. Whatever poetical descriptions we may find, 'supreme luminous regions, middle sky, third heaven, lap of the red dawns,' the pleasures of the Fathers are essentially mundane ones: rivers of mead, milk and waters, pools of butter with banks of honey, also Apsarases or celestial damsels.

The dead were happy; their life was worthy

[1] Oldenberg (tr. V. Henry), *Religion du Véda*, pp. 453, 457.

to be lived. The men of these old Āryan days might have said what the philosophers said later: "Man has three births: he is born from his mother, reborn in the person of his son, and he finds his highest birth in death."

While the ascetic—the learned ascetic—does not expect anything from the gods or fear anything from the demons, with the old Āryas happiness in this life depends on the goodwill of the gods and the deprecation of malignant spirits. A. Barth said eloquently[1]: "The connexion between man and the gods is conceived as a very close one. Always and everywhere he feels that he is in their hands and that all his movements are under their eye. They are masters close at hand, who exact tasks of him and to whom he owes constant homage. He must be humble, for he is weak and they are strong; he must be sincere towards them, for they cannot be deceived. Nay, he knows that they in turn do not deceive, and that they have a right to require his confidence as a friend, a brother, a father....Sacrifice is often an act of affection and gratitude towards the gods, through which man acknowledges their sovereignty, renders thanks to

[1] *Religions of India*, p. 35 foll.

them for their benefits and hopes to obtain others in the future either in this life or after death."

The Vedic gods, except in a few instances, are not regarded as 'transcendent'; to a certain extent, they depend on man. As the dead are fed by funeral oblations, so the gods need sacrificial oblations. A. Barth continues: "In the grossest sense, sacrifice is a mere bargain. Man needs things which the god possesses, such as rain, light, warmth and health, while the god is hungry and seeks offerings from man; there is giving and receiving on both sides: 'As at a stipulated price, let us exchange force and vigour, O Indra! Give me and I shall give thee; bring me, and I shall bring thee.'"

Malignant spirits, if not in the Rigveda itself, at least in the Vedic religion, are no less important than the gods. All the movements of daily life as well as all the ceremonies of religion are to be made safe from their attacks. Illnesses and mishaps of every description are their work. Therefore they must be propitiated, and it is an old formula that "every supernatural being (*yakṣa*) has a right to his own offering."

III

Such were the fundamental ideas of the Āryan religion and life. The Ārya, without being δεισιδαιμονέστερος, did love and respect his gods; he used meat and even cow's flesh; he sacrificed to obtain male offspring and a life of a hundred autumns; he hoped after death to join the Fathers and to enjoy, with them, the offerings of his sons. Life is serene, joyful, active, not in any way spiritual or intellectual.

One sees how radical a change was necessary for asceticism and the disciplines of salvation to be possible. The inborn feelings of the Āryas had to be destroyed to make room for an altogether different conception of life and human destiny.

What were the causes of this change? They certainly were many and manifold.

To begin with, we must not forget that the Sanskrit-speaking people, the priestly and feudal aristocracy who created the disciplines of salvation, were no longer of unmixed Āryan race, as the old poets of the Veda, but a mixture of Āryas and of the aborigines. Oldenberg has laid much stress on this fact: we should not venture, in our present state of knowledge, to base too much upon it. But it is certain that the 'intellectual'

Āryas, at the time of the compilation of the Rigveda and later on, did not see and feel as their ancestors did. They had acquired, as A. Barth says, "a love of mystery, an extreme subtlety of mind, a fearlessness of inconsequences and absurdities," together with the *sérieux*, the disinterestedness and the strength of mystical research that are, through history, such prominent marks of the Hindu mind.

On the other hand, this aristocracy was likely to borrow from the aborigines, and from the mass of the Āryan people in daily contact with the aborigines, many superstitions or beliefs—confused notions connected with penance, ecstasy, reincarnations—as well as the principle of *ahiṃsā*, 'respect for life'; a sort of cult of the cow; new gods, obscene and cruel; phallic worship; idolatry, and so on. Such notions, it is certain they borrowed: this can be proved in many cases.

But however profound and large the influence of new ethnic and climatic surroundings, the Sanskrit-speaking people, especially the Brahmans, were the heirs and the faithful preservers of the Āryan tradition and mind. The notions they borrowed were at once elaborated into rationalistic and fairly coherent doctrines. That again may be proved in many cases, and we shall quote an instance which is of special interest for us. The belief in reincarnations was a purely savage surmise, liable to be organized into what is called totemism, an unprogressive and absurd paganism, and no more: to be sure of it, we have only to open the books of Tylor or Durckheim. Brahmans and Buddhists borrowed this belief, which was altogether new to the Āryan tradition; but they found no difficulty in adapting it either to the dogma of the reward of good and evil deeds, or to a monism as rigid as that of the Eleatic school.

The change we are studying is, to a large extent, not a revolution, but an evolution; and the safest way to understand it is perhaps to describe it as an autonomous alteration of the genuine Āryan beliefs and notions. The Brahmans, endowed with an equal genius for conservation and adaptation, were the workers of the change.

A word on the Brahmans and their probable origin.

The old rites of the family, offerings to the domestic fire, had, in the beginning and for a long time, no professional priest. The father and the mother were the priests at their fire[1]. But a certain ritual, which is as old as the period when the ancestors of the Iranians and of the Vedic Indians lived together, the ritual of

[1] P. Oltramare, *Le rôle du Yajamāna dans le sacrifice.*

Soma-Haoma, had from of old a clergy of its own. And, by a slow progress, the members of certain clans, better provided than others with technical knowledge in formulas and in rites, became the masters of the altar and the acknowledged intermediaries between gods and men. They were the ancestors of the Brahmans.

The Brahmans were, by profession, busied with gods, sacrifice, and ritual. After a time, before even the Rigveda was compiled, they became philosophers and they made many striking discoveries. Four are worthy of notice.

1. The most ancient, if not the most important: the traditional gods are not the self-existent and individual beings whom the poets of old praised so ardently.

Each of them had long been credited with the features and the characteristic powers of his colleagues—the so-called 'henotheism,' which is not, as Max Müller said, a stage in the making of the gods, but, on the contrary, a stage towards their disintegration.

Polytheism pure and simple was not crushed, and it remains as living in the India of to-day as it was thirty centuries ago; but another theology crept behind and below it, and was admitted, first among thinkers, then by the great public, as an esoteric and more scientific view of the universe.

The gods, the gods we know, are not real gods. Who then is the true god, the unknown god? The texts permit us to trace different lines in the development of the theological inquiry.

We meet sometimes in the Veda lofty expressions of a moral monotheism,—and, throughout history, they are re-echoed from time to time. Varuṇa, for instance, is more than once a sort of Jehovah of the Far East: he has established the sun and made a path for it; it is in accordance with his order or his rule that the moon and the stars go their changeless course; he loves truth and hates iniquity; he pardons the sinner who repents. But there is no evidence that this monotheism is a product of philosophical speculation; we are inclined to think that it is rather the spontaneous expression of religious feeling, a devotion rather than a doctrine. As a matter of fact, the theology of the later Veda tends to become a pallid deism, coupled with pantheistic tendencies which become stronger as time goes on.

The true god is a generator, an architect of the cosmos, as were the majority of the old gods, each in his turn ('henotheism'). But the changes in the divine nomenclature show the evolution of the philosophical thought. Instead of Agni, the omnipresent but visible fire, or Indra, holder of the thunderbolt, or Varuṇa, 'who is the ocean and is contained in a drop of water,' the Vedic poets now prefer new names, Prajāpati, the Lord of creatures, Viśvakarman, the fabricator of the universe, the great Asura or Great Spirit, Svayambhū, the self-existing Being, Parameṣṭhin, the Supreme.

Little personality is attached to these gods, who have no history as Indra or Heracles has, and who are not 'natural gods' as the Fire or the Sky. While the old gods, the gods of the sacrifice, the heavenly heroes endowed with cosmical powers, *les dieux à biographie*, fade before them, they themselves appear as mere shadows of a more abstruse reality, or rather as the mere names of an impersonal anonymous force, a universal principle.

"The gods are only one single Being under different names,"

ekaṃ sad viprā bahudhā vadanti.

Is this Being a god or a force? Is the universe born from a principle possessed of name and form (*sat*), or from a liquid and undifferentiated mass (*asat*)? Did the gods come first and the universe afterwards? The poet professes to ignore the right answer: "The god that is above knows it, or he does not know"; but the real thought of the poet is not doubtful: the primeval force is styled Heat, Order, Truth, Waters, Golden Germ (first born of the Waters), Kāma or Desire, the starting point in the evolution of being, Kāla or Time, creator and destroyer, or, with a name which is destined to have a marvellous fortune, Brahman.

Brahman is a new god, but an old word: it meant prayer or sacred formula. How did the word acquire a new meaning of this kind? Because the sacred formula came to be regarded as the great creative power.

2. While speculation on the gods and on cosmogony leads to the substitution, for the divine heroes of yore, of abstract and obscure forces, the speculation on sacrifice leads to a like result.

Victor Henry is inclined to believe that the Indo-Iranian sacrifice of Soma-Haoma, from which the Vedic sacrifice of Soma is derived, was originally a magical rite for rain. This view is only a conjecture. But two points seem to be ascertained. (1) While magical notions are always lurking in old rituals, the oldest theologians of the Veda—the authors of the Hymns—

saw in the sacrifice of Soma more than a mere act of oblation: "To sacrifice is to stir up, actually to beget, two divinities of first rank, the two principles of life *par excellence*, Agni, the Fire, and Soma, the Oblation[1]." (2) On the other hand, the magical conception of sacrifice was, for a long time and to a large extent, checked by the lofty idea the Āryan had of his gods. Later on this conception underwent an enormous development in the circle of the professional sacrificers.

Indians—sorcerers, priests, philosophers or poets—are not a little ambitious: *ils voient grand*. The Vedic priests ventured to think that their hymns, formulae and rites were, not only the invigorating power that helps the gods in the struggle for light and waters, but "the condition even of the normal course of things." Sacrifice prevents the world from lapsing into chaos. Further, if sacrifice is the actual cosmical agency, it must probably at the beginning have been the cosmogonical factor. It was by sacrifice that the gods delivered the world from chaos; it was by sacrifice that the gods became immortal, and why should not Man also become immortal by sacrifice?

[1] Barth, *Religions*, *loc. cit.*

Sacrifice to whom? To no one. Rites and formulae are, in themselves, efficient.

In short, the universe was conceived as a huge ritual, the quintessence of which is the Veda, the eternal and productive Word. Vāc, the Voice, is praised in some passages as another Logos, but this Logos is magical sound, not reason.

3. The fading away of the living gods, the rise of pantheistic gods, the mechanical conception of a cosmic sacrifice,—all these transformations of the old ideology went hand in hand with another and possibly more important transformation. The beliefs concerning the destiny of Man were utterly modified. The Vedic Indians discovered—step by step—the doctrine of transmigration (*saṃsāra*).

How they made this discovery, that the Fathers die in the heaven whither they have been brought by funeral ceremonies, that the dead are reborn as men or as animals, that animals may be reborn as men—how they came to accept these ideas which were as foreign to their ancestors and to their sacred folk-lore as they are to us—is a long history[1]. It is the history of a radical change in mental and

[1] See A. M. Boyer, 'Étude sur l'origine de la doctrine du Saṃsāra,' *J. As.* 1901, I, p. 451.

moral habits. We shall only point out some of the doctrinal factors that seem to have been decisive.

The starting point is the admission of the 're-death' (*punarmṛtyu*) of the dead. Death was deemed no less powerful a force than Desire or Time. There is a multiplicity of deadly forces which pursue Man everywhere, some in the worlds on this side, some in the worlds beyond. Therefore the dead, although they are made half-divine, die again.

On the other hand, the philosophers, who dared to inquire into the origin of the gods and the universe, could not be long satisfied with the traditional eschatology. Could they admit that the Fathers possess, for ever, a perfect happiness, enjoying every pleasure of a magnified human life? "Whatever Man attains, he desires to go beyond it; if he should reach heaven itself, he would desire to go beyond it." An eternal paradise of Mahomet or a Walhalla seems unlikely to a philosophical mind; it would be, in any case, an altogether wrong paradise, as says Andrew Lang, for philosophers.

4. The speculation, which has in this way dispelled or abandoned the hope of immortality, cannot stop at this conclusion. It is everywhere

the rôle of philosophy to destroy natural beliefs, and to rebuild them according to some new pattern. This second task of a philosophy the Vedic philosophy did not fail to fulfil.

Psychology began. The following distinction was made.

There is, on the one hand, the body with the vital energies that seem in a closer relation with the body, and which savages often explain by a number of souls. There is, on the other hand, the truly living principle (*jīva*) that constitutes the true self of Man. This principle, which is an entity, really a 'noumenon,' is called either *puruṣa*, 'man,' 'spirit,' or *ātman*, etymologically 'breath' (?), literally 'Self,' the reflexive pronoun and the noun.

The *puruṣa* or *ātman* is eternal. It has inhabited various bodies and is destined to inhabit new ones; but its natural aim is to reach an eternal, changeless abode; free from any created or generated body, it will live by itself, either conscious or unconscious, either formless or wrapped in a form of its own, according to the preferences of the philosophers. There have been many diverging conceptions of the Self.

But the solution, which is by far the most

popular among the Brahmans, is to identify the Self with the universal god then in process of discovery, with Brahman.

The inquiry as to the gods and the universe has shown that the true god is a nameless, universal agent, the self or breath of the world. Therefore the god who blows in the wind and shines in the sun is the same principle that breathes through the human mouth and keeps the living body warm. The universal self is the true self of Man, as it is the life and the essence of Nature: "It directs the eye and the ear; it is the ear of the ear, the mind of the mind, the breath of the breath, the speech of the speech, the eye of the eye." "This Breath (*ātman*) is the guardian of the world, the Lord of the world: he is my Self."

Such an admission: "I am that Being," "I am Brahman," was a bold and a decisive move. In short, that was the great discovery which has remained for at least twenty-five centuries the capital and the most cherished truth of the Indian people. It is much more than an academical theory.

There is only one Self, for the self of man is not a creation, an emanation or a part of the

Self of the universe: it is this very Self. "The unique and indivisible Self is immortal, happy, unqualified, unconscious; but he animates the body, he becomes, as it were, man. As such he experiences pain and desire, he accumulates merit and demerit, he migrates from existence to existence, always unhappy because he is always a prey to ever recurring death,—and without any hope of deliverance, as long as he does not withdraw himself from the not Self. But as soon as the individualized Self has acquired the perfect immediate certainty that he is the universal Self, he no longer experiences doubt, desire or suffering. He still acts, as the wheel of the potter continues to revolve when the potter has ceased to turn it. Death, at last, abolishes what no longer exists for him, the last appearance of duality[1]."

That is perfect bliss,—which we sometimes experience in dreamless sleep, when the Self is withdrawn from not Self,—and unconsciousness: for, "where there is a duality, one can see the other, one can smell the other, one can address the other, one can hear the other, one can think of the other, one can grasp the other. But where for each everything has turned into his

[1] A. Barth, *Religions of India*, p. 78. See below, p. 161.

own self, by whom and whom shall he see, smell, address, hear, think or grasp[1]?"

That the doctrines of transmigration, of the Self, of the merging of the individual self in the great self, were antagonistic to the traditional beliefs in the gods, the sacrifice, the paradises, and aimed directly at the destruction of the whole fabric of social life, is self-evident.

The times were ripe for asceticism and the disciplines of deliverance to arise.

[1] *Bṛhadāraṇyaka*, II, 4, 13; compare IV, 3, 23.

CHAPTER II

THE BUDDHIST SOUL

I. Buddhism a form of rationalism. II. Buddhist psychology; contradictions. III. There is no Self: Man is a chariot. IV. There is reward of actions in a future life. V. Whether Buddhists deny rebirth or migration of a soul, while maintaining migration of *karman* or character. VI. Buddhists admit a sort of soul.

I

We have given a general definition of the Indian disciplines of salvation and tried to make clear that they are Paths leading the ascetic, beyond the ocean of transmigration, to some mysterious somewhere. Buddhism has been, from the beginning, a religion, a religion properly so called; that is, there have been, from the beginning, Buddhists for whom Buddha was a god and who did not hope for a better state than rebirth in Buddha's heaven; but this Buddhist religion has nothing or little to do with the most authentic teaching of Śākyamuni. Old Buddhism is essentially a discipline of salvation,—and this discipline widely differs from the other disciplines of salvation.

If we were asked to characterise in a word the

old Buddhist discipline of salvation and the old Buddhism as a whole, we should say that it is a form of rationalism. Every idea and every practice made use of by Śākyamuni to build up his theory and his rule of religious life have been freed from any tinge of mysticism.

Four points may be distinguished.

1. The most conspicuous and 'buddhistic' feature of Buddhist rationalism is the definition Śākyamuni and his disciples give of Man. Man is to be delivered from transmigration; but what do we mean by the word 'man'? Much depends on the answer, which will be studied in this chapter.

2. As concerns transmigration and the factors that govern transmigration, the rivals of Śākyamuni believe that God, or the gods, or destiny, or sacrifice are of greater or less importance. Śākyamuni, on the contrary, teaches that transmigration depends on the actions of Man himself[1].

3. As concerns the aim to be reached, deliverance. For the rivals of Śākyamuni, deliverance is either the merging of the individual Self in the great Self, or some mystical state of the Self; while Śākyamuni takes a merely negative view of deliverance: the Buddhist deliverance or Nirvāṇa is only cessation of rebirth, end of misery[2].

[1] See chapters III and IV. [2] See chapter V.

4. As concerns the Path leading to deliverance, the rivals of Śākyamuni lay much stress on sacrifice, penance, ecstasies, esoteric wisdom, as means to deliverance. With Śākyamuni, the essential part of the Path is the understanding of a few very simple truths: 'Life ends in death,' 'Everything is misery[1].'

We say that old Buddhism was rationalistic, thoroughly rationalistic; but this thoroughness was not absolute, and could not be absolute. This fact must be borne in mind, even when the rationalistic character of Buddhism is emphasized, if we are to avoid the mistake of some historians who describe the old Buddhists according to the pattern of the agnostics or the materialists of to-day.

Buddhism originated in pagan and mystical surroundings. It is true that it succeeded in explaining the cosmos and human destiny without having recourse to any metaphysical agent; that it succeeded in making all the popular beliefs—belief in transmigration, in paradises, in hells, in magical powers—and nearly all the ascetic practices—penances and ecstasies—subservient to its own rationalistic ideals and principles.

[1] See chapter VI.

But it did not reject these beliefs, it did not contest the efficacy of these practices: these beliefs and these practices are, in fact, essential parts of the Buddhist doctrine.

Buddhism, therefore—we mean the Buddhism of the Books and of the most learned monks—is a rationalism, but a qualified, an Indian rationalism.

Moreover, this rationalism is not always consistent with itself. A number of inconsistencies might be quoted. For example the teaching of the Master was strict on the point that merit is strictly personal. But old India believed that merit, together with its reward, is something that can be given by one individual to another. A doctrine of the transfer of merit was tacitly lurking in some Buddhist circles and found expression in several passages of the Scripture. We are told that the right means of helping the dead is not to give them offerings, but to make gifts to the living for the benefit of the dead; that the right means of rendering homage to the deities is not to worship them, but to give them a share in our own pious works. Later this doctrine of the transfer of merit became the leading idea of neo-Buddhism (Mahāyāna) and was developed into a dogma comparable, in many respects, to the Christian dogma of the communion of saints.

II

The Buddhist definition of Man is summarized in a word, *nairātmya*, 'selflessness,' not, as usually translated, 'soullessness.' The matter is somewhat difficult, the more so because we do not agree with the common opinion of scholars, and we cannot avoid discussing this opinion.

Two facts are well ascertained and beyond discussion: (1) Śākyamuni does not admit the existence of a Self (*ātman*), a permanent individual; he teaches that the so-called Self is a compound of material and spiritual data called *skandhas*; (2) but he nevertheless teaches reward of actions in a future life. There is, *prima facie*, a contradiction.

The common explanation of this contradiction is as follows: Śākyamuni teaches annihilation at death, and denies rebirth or transmigration; but he believes that, owing to the strength of actions, a new being is created who is to inherit the actions of the dead man and to enjoy their fruit. A man dies and is dead for ever, but his goodness or wickedness persists and causes another man to be born.

We shall show, to the best of our power, that this explanation lacks the support of the texts and is inadmissible; and we shall set forth the doctrine which is clearly delineated by the Buddhists themselves—not, it is true, by the oldest Buddhists. There is not a Self, a permanent substantial unity, but there is a person, to be described as 'a living continuous fluid complex,' which does not remain quite the same for two consecutive moments, but which continues for an endless number of existences, bridging an endless number of deaths, without becoming completely different from itself.

III

The primitive psychology, in India as elsewhere, was 'animistic.'

There is a principle of life and heat, which moves the body, feels and wills. This principle, although it is often identified with the breath (*prāṇa*), is not a spiritual entity. Rather is it a semi-material soul, or an impalpable body—a 'subtle body' (*sūkṣma śarīra*) as the Indians say—a double which, during life, may abandon the gross body, its fleshly abode, when for instance it travels far away in dreams; and which, at death, finally flies away by an aperture at the top of the head, only to be reincarnated elsewhere.

The Brahmans started from these 'animistic' views to develop a metaphysical psychology, quite different from the theories of the West. It must never be forgotten that the Indian philosopher found his materials, not in Nature, through a direct and scientific observation, but in the crude surmises of the popular or ritualistic tradition. A strong and truly philosophical thought came into contact, not with real and ascertained facts, but with wild speculations. The result is often somewhat bewildering.

The leading principle of the philosopher was that what is transitory cannot be the Self. He therefore distinguished two constituents. The first one is the subtle body of the old 'animistic' belief: subtle elements, subtle earth, water, wind and fire, making subtle organs of sensation, one of which is the mind. The second constituent is an everlasting and spiritual principle, the Self that is enveloped in the subtle body, in the semi-material soul.

On the nature of the Self the Brahmans do not agree. Two schools are prominent, the Sāṃkhya and the Vedānta.

According to Sāṃkhya, there are many Selves,

called *puruṣa*, a word which means Man. They are eternal, unmodifiable and passive, producing nothing and doing nothing; they are enveloped in the subtle body; they illuminate the play of the senses and of the mind; they experience pleasure and disgust; they migrate from existence to existence "until the day when, fully satiated and recognising themselves as distinct from matter, they break partnership with it and return to their primeval liberty and unconsciousness[1]." The Self has no longer anything to illuminate.

With the second school or Vedānta, there is only one Self, the great, unique and unmodifiable Self, another name of which is Brahman. This unique Self becomes multiform in appearance, owing to the diversity of the material envelopes in which it is wrapped; these envelopes—as well as the whole cosmos—are the creation, the 'magic' of the Self; but it does not know. When it knows, the illusions come to an end and the Self is delivered from individuality and from pain.

In both these systems, the Self is, as the philosophers say, transcendent to the psychical life. For Sāṃkhya, the Self is only a light that illuminates the play of senses and mind, which

[1] Barth, *Religions of India*, p. 70.

are material and by themselves unconscious; for Vedānta, only a magician who takes interest in the magical shows that he unwillingly creates; for Sāṃkhya and Vedānta, 'ideation' is exterior to the Self. The question is whether it is not possible to dispense with such a Self. Śākyamuni answers in the affirmative.

The Buddhist psychology, in sharp contrast with Brahman psychologies—and, it may be said, with nearly all psychologies—avoids or pretends to avoid any metaphysical surmise. It is built up of facts, of the facts that seemed, in that old time, to be scientifically ascertained. And it is a surprise that, but for one point—transmigration—the theory concocted by the yellow-garbed monks of yore agrees closely with one of the modern theories of the soul, the theory of Hume or Taine and of many scientists.

According to the Buddhists, no Self, that is, no unity, permanent feeling or thinking entity, comes into the field of inquiry. We know only the body, which is visibly a composite, growing and decaying thing, and a number of phenomena, feelings, perceptions, wishes or wills, cognitions—in philosophic language, a number of states of consciousness. That these states of consciousness depend upon a Self, are the product of a Self or arise in a Self, is only a surmise, since there is no consciousness of a Self outside these states of consciousness; and a wrong surmise, since there cannot be connexion between 'being' and 'becoming': "There are perceptions, but we do not know a perceiver."

As a matter of fact, we are well aware of the origin of perceptions, of the origin of all the states of consciousness.

There is an organism, a physico-psychical organism. On the one hand, the gross body, with the five gross organs, eye and so on. On the other hand, the subtle body, that is, the five true organs, subtle eye and so on, and the intellectual organ, the mind: an organ, made of subtle matter like the visual organ, which knows ideas as the visual organ sees colours.

There are exterior objects which are brought into contact with this organism.

Thus arises consciousness[1]: "The colour blue being given, the organ of the eye being also given, there arises a contact which originates a visual knowledge, namely a blue image." This image is at once elaborated by the mind which

[1] See *Saṃyutta*, II, p. 72; *Majjhima*, I, III; *Milinda*, p. 56 and *passim*.

creates an intellectual or mental knowledge in giving a name to the object: "that is blue."

Hence follows a sensation, pleasant or unpleasant, which produces desire or disgust, which in turn produces an act of volition, an action. Buddha is reported to have said that "there is action, but there is not an agent."

A very bold statement, but a very logical one. For what the heretics, that is the Brahmans, call a Self is not an individual, but a complex of elements, some of which are material (*rūpa*) and gross—the visible body—some of which are material and subtle—the organs properly so-called—some of which are non-material (*arūpin*)—the states of consciousness, feeling, naming, will, cognition. Man is made of these elements (*skandhas*)[1]; he is a compound; and no compound can be an individual, a being.

This position, denial of any entity—a soul—"which gives unity and permanence to what we call the individual," is to be justified by intricate speculations, both in the East, with the Buddhists, and in the West, with our modern psychologists. But it is very simple in itself, and was made intelligible to any one by similes.

[1] For technical definitions see *Abhidharmakośa* III and Mrs Rhys Davids, *Psychology*, 1914, p. 40 foll.

The best known is the simile of the chariot; it is referred to in our oldest documents (Saṃyutta), and it is explained at length in the 'Questions of King Milinda' (Milindapañha), a collection of dialogues between a Buddhist sage, Nāgasena, and the King Menander, one of the successors of Alexander in the Far East, sovereign of North West India in the second century B.C. There are some reasons to believe that this *enfant perdu* of Hellenism was converted to Buddhism; and his conversion began as follows:

Milinda asks: "What is your name?"

"I am known as Nāgasena; but Nāgasena is only a term, appellation, designation, mere name, mere empty sound, for there an individual does not exist."

"But," says Milinda, "if the individual does not exist, who is it then who furnishes you monks with robes, food and so on? Who is it who keeps the precepts of Buddha? Who is it who abandons these precepts and commits sin? In that case, if there is no individual, there is no merit, no demerit; neither is he a murderer who kills a monk, nor can you, monks, have any teacher or preceptor or ordination. Do answer me, are not your nails, teeth, skin, flesh Nāgasena? are not your body, feelings, sensations, volitions, cognitions Nāgasena?"

Nāgasena answers in the negative and Milinda concludes: "You speak a falsehood, a lie"; for, when one speaks of Nāgasena one has in view the body of Nāgasena: "Nāgasena is fat or tall," and the 'soul' of Nāgasena: "Nāgasena is wise, Nāgasena strives for Nirvāṇa."

Milinda is now to be questioned in his turn: "You

are of noble birth, prince, and if you walk in the middle of the day on hot sandy ground, it is very bad for your feet, your body and your mind. Pray, did you come on foot or in a chariot?"—"I came in a chariot." —"If you came in a chariot, explain to me what a chariot is. Is the pole the chariot?"

Milinda confesses that neither the pole, nor the axle, nor the wheels, nor the frame, nor the yoke, nor any part of the chariot is the chariot; and Nāgasena concludes: "When you said: 'I came in a chariot,' you spoke a falsehood, a lie; there is no chariot[1]."

For, as it is said elsewhere:

Just as the word 'chariot' is but a mode of expression for axle, wheels, and other constituent members, placed in a certain relation to each other; but, when we come to examine the members one by one, we discover that, in an absolute sense, there is no chariot; just as the words 'house,' 'fist,' 'lute,' 'army,' 'city,' 'tree,' are only modes of expression for collections of certain things disposed in a certain manner, in exactly the same way, the words 'living being' and 'ego' are only modes of expression for a complex of bodily and non-bodily constituents[2].

The problem of the whole and the parts (*avayava*, *avayavin*) has been, in India, the topic of long and abstruse discussions. The Buddhists maintain that the whole is only an *être de raison*; their opponents are as clever as they are. That

[1] *Milinda*, p. 25, Rhys Davids, I (*S.B.E.* xxxv), p. 40; Warren, *Buddhism in translations*, p. 129; E. J. Thomas, *Buddhist Scriptures*, (Wisdom of the East Series), p. 118.

[2] *Visuddhimagga*, apud Warren, p. 133.

this problem is a real one, not a mere logomachy, is made clear by the following remark which well summarizes Nāgasena's thought: "If you infer an entity behind an individual man, you must also logically infer it behind every individual thing, such as a chariot. Buddhists reject both entities, and Plato equally logically accepts both," when he recognizes in a bed "the existence of some one Form, which includes the numerous particular things to which we apply the same name" (*Rep.* x)[1].

But it may be urged that, among the constituents of the Self, there is a constituent which is likely to be the very Self: the mind or thought or consciousness, the thing that exerts itself, that keeps the memory of its feelings and exertions.

Śākyamuni was well aware of this objection, and he scornfully rejects it[2].

Men, in general, even the non-Buddhists, willingly agree that this body, composed of the four elements, earth, water, air and fire, is not the Self; they easily divest themselves of passion for it: the increase and the wasting away of the body are manifest enough. "But that, O monks, which is called mind, thought, consciousness, here the non-Buddhist sees his own Self, and he

[1] E. J. Thomas, *Buddhist Scriptures*, p. 119.
[2] *Saṃyutta*, II, p. 94.

is incapable of divesting himself of passion for it. Why do I say so? Because, from time immemorial, from the beginning of transmigration which is without beginning, the non-Buddhist has held, cherished and loved this notion: 'this is mine, this I am, this is my Self.' But it is less foolish to consider the body composed of the four elements as a Self, rather than the mind. Why do I say so? Because it is evident, O monks, that this body lasts for one year, for two, three, four, five, ten, twenty, thirty, forty, fifty years, lasts for a hundred years and even more. But that, O monks, which is called mind, thought, consciousness, keeps up an incessant round, by day and by night, of perishing as one thing and springing up as another."

The conclusion that seems to be forced upon us has been vividly drawn by Rhys Davids[1]:

Śākyamuni acknowledged the reality of the emotional and intellectual dispositions, but he refused absolutely to look upon them as a unity. The position is so absolute, so often insisted on, so fundamental to the right understanding of primitive Buddhism that it is essential there should be no mistake about it. Yet the position is also so original, so fundamentally opposed to what is usually understood as religious belief, both in India and elsewhere, that there is great temptation to attempt to find a loophole through which at least a covert or esoteric belief in a soul, and in the future life (that is of course of a soul), can be recognized, in some sort of way, as part of so widely accepted a religious system. There is no loophole, and the efforts to find one have always met with unswerving opposition both in the Scriptures (Piṭakas) themselves and in extra-canonical works.

[1] *Dialogues of the Buddha*, I, p. 189.

IV

Are we to admit this conclusion?

If Man is a chariot, if there is no soul, there is no free will, no responsibility, no sin, no merit, no future life, no reward of actions in a future life. The remarks of Menander hold good. But it is an ascertained fact that, from the beginning, Buddhism waged an obstinate war against the materialists or unbelievers, the Nāstikas, that is, the philosophers who say: "It is not," who deny the reward of good actions and the punishment of bad ones in a future life.

We shall see[1] that these unbelievers were numerous at the time of Śākyamuni—an epoch of philosophic analysis—and that Śākyamuni, who is as a rule described as a denier of soul, may be more exactly described as a strong maintainer of responsibility and future life. He said:

> To say that Man, when the body dissolves, is cut off, perishes, does not exist any longer, that is heresy, heretical belief, heretical jungle, heretical wilderness.

It is more than a heresy; it is the heresy; it is what is called technically 'wrong view'

[1] See below, p. 61.

(*mithyādṛṣṭi*), the most dangerous and wicked among human errors and sins[1] as it is destructive of all morality, and precipitates the unbeliever into hell: "You say that there is no future life. Well! the executioners of Yama, the king and the judge of the dead, will soon change your opinion on the matter."

So much for the dogmatic evidences.

On the other hand, the texts which affirm the reward of actions, and the personal character of this reward, are innumerable. There are hundreds of Birth stories, Jātakas, legendary and moral tales, stories of the days of yore: all end in the same stereotyped sentences with the so-called identification of the characters: "What do you think, O monks?—says Buddha—I was then the wise white elephant, Devadatta was the wicked hunter."

Elsewhere:

> Ānanda—the beloved disciple—has committed such an act. Who will enjoy the fruit of this act but Ānanda?

But the most emphatic affirmation of the

[1] To believe in a Self is a heresy (*dṛṣṭi*), the *śāśvata-* or *satkāya-dṛṣṭi*; but is not a sin. Heresy prevents the acquisition of holiness and of Nirvāṇa, but does not prevent the acquisition of merit. A believer in the Self may be reborn as a god and even as Brahmā. On the contrary, the denial of the reward of actions in a future life is a sin, just as murder, theft, etc.

that effect. But the Buddhist added, from the beginning, that there is no annihilation, cutting off (*uccheda*), because—as it was soon ascertained—if the being who revives is not the same as the old one, it is not, on the other hand, different from the old one.

That seems a queer statement, but, in the words of the Brahman when explaining intricate mysteries to his wife, "we are not to be perplexed at this statement, it is really very simple." In any case, it is quite Buddhist.

The problem of the non-identity of the 'new' being with the previous one, is only a special instance of the general rule of existence.

Existence is transformation (*anyathābhāva*). What is called a being is a complex of different constituents, a chariot: that is the static point of view. But a being is also a series (*saṃtāna*) of successive states, originating in dependence; a being is a fire or a plant. This point of view, which may be styled dynamic, is to be traced in the Scriptures and is frequently insisted on in the scholastic texts.

When milk is turned into curds, the non-identity, the non-permanence (*śāśvata*) is evident: curds are not milk. But, as a matter of fact, there is no 'interruption' (*uccheda*), because there has been an incessant and gradual change in milk, long before it was curds, even when it seemed to be the same milk[1].

In the same way, Man is a living continuous complex, which does not remain quite the same for two consecutive moments, but which continues for an endless number of existences without becoming completely different from itself[2].

If we consider a man at two different moments of his present life, it is safe to say that he is not the same; but is it not equally evident that he is not another?

The 'murderer' whom the executioners lead to the scaffold is not a 'murderer,' for he is not the same man who has committed murder; but he merits punishment because he cannot be said to be another than the murderer, being the 'continuation' of the murderer. The girl is not the child; but she nevertheless belongs to the man to whom she has been married when a child and who has paid the dowry. The father of the girl has not the right of giving the girl to a new husband for a new dowry, because the girl is the 'continuation' of the child[3].

In the same way, the being who is to enjoy

[1] Warren, *Buddhism in Translations*, p. 237.

[2] *Mahāniddesa*, p 117; *Visuddhimagga*, VIII (Warren, p. 150).

[3] *Milinda*, p. 46 foll.; Warren, p. 236; E. J. Thomas, *Buddhist Scriptures*, p. 123.

the fruit of the acts of a dead man is the continuation of the dead man.

Here is a good simile[1].

Let us imagine a jungle, bounded by a river, and a fire that is burning this jungle. As a matter of fact we have no right to speak of a fire, as if it were a unity. There is only a succession of flames; each of them lasts only for a moment and dies together with the fuel it consumes at the very place where it is born; but these flames are generated in succession and strictly depending one upon another, although the fuel they consume is spread over a large space. This fire, burning a jungle bounded by a river, provides us with an exact image of the life of a man during one existence. The physico-psychical life does not depend upon a living principle (*jīva*) or a Self; in itself it is not a something; it is lacking both in substance and in unity; it is only a series of physical states and of states of consciousness generated in succession, depending one upon another, although each of them lasts only for a moment.

Now suppose that, owing to the strength of the wind, a fire were to appear across the river, in another jungle, at the moment when the first

[1] The first part is from *Abhidharma* sources.

fire is dying on the nearer bank of the river. One cannot say that the fire has crossed the river; one cannot say that the fire in the new jungle is not the very fire that has burned the first jungle: in an absolute sense, there is not one fire, there are not two fires; a fire does not exist independently of the flames. In an absolute sense, we are concerned with one succession of flames, and it is evident that this succession has not been interrupted (*ucchinna*) by the river, in the same way as it was not interrupted when it developed in the jungle itself. The fact is that, but for the wind, this succession would have been cut off on the nearer bank; but, owing to the strength of the wind, a certain number of flames has been created, forming as it were a bridge between the two banks.

That simile gives us an image of a living series extending over two or many different existences. Owing to the strength of the wind of actions, the ultimate state of consciousness in an existence—that is the consciousness of the dying man, the death-consciousness (*maraṇāntika vijñāna*)—begets or rather inaugurates a short series of states of consciousness (coupled with a subtle organism), the last of which takes up its abode in some matrix (*pratisaṃdhivijñāna*).

It is in this way that the Buddhist scholastic has solved the riddle and understood one of the clearest statements of Śākyamuni: "If the consciousness were not to descend into the maternal womb, the new being, body and mind, would not arise."

How is therefore to be understood the Buddhist doctrine of 'selflessness'? Does it mean that there is no soul and no future life of a soul? Certainly so, if we have in view a metaphysical entity, a soul which is sometimes looking through the senses, as so many windows, sometimes busied with itself, sometimes asleep; a soul which, without being itself subject to change, is apt to take a new abode when the body dissolves. The Buddhists do not admit any soul of this kind, for, according to them, it would be master of its sensations and feelings[1]; but, in its stead, they recognize a living complex, a continuous fluid complex both bodily and mental, a person which, in fact, possesses nearly all the characters of a soul as we understand the word: it continues through many existences eating the fruit of its acts; it controls itself; it makes exertions to reach a better state; it may, when it is sublimized

[1] *Vinaya Texts*, I, p. 100 foll.

by appropriate exertions, abandon its bodily constituents and live for centuries in some immaterial heaven as a pure spirit.

But this person is not a substance and it is therefore capable of dissolution. This dissolution is 'deliverance' or Nirvāṇa: the series of the states of consciousness is interrupted at death when desire and action have been destroyed, just as the fire dies on the nearer bank of the river when there is no wind.

CHAPTER III

BUDDHIST DEFINITION OF KARMAN

I. Introductory. II. Ancient history of Karman. III. Karman is volition and voluntary action. IV. Karman is moral action.

I

The Buddhist 'soul,' a series of physico-psychical states, would come to an end at death, when the physical organism dissolves, but for the strength of the actions which are to be enjoyed in a future life by a new physico-psychical apparatus, a continuation of the first one.

Action, in Sanskrit, *karman*, is one of the Indian words that the theosophists and the neo-Buddhists have made known in the West. We must feel grateful for it. For we can say shortly 'doctrine of Karman,' meaning all the speculations concerned with action, and especially the dogma of the ripening (*vipāka*) of action.

The doctrine of Karman is more than the belief in the reward of good actions and the punishment of bad ones, here below or in another life; such a belief is a very common one and has nothing specifically Indian.

The doctrine of Karman presupposes the belief in transmigration and is primarily a rationalistic and moral explanation of the variety of the conditions of living beings through many consecutive existences.

By a rationalistic and moral explanation, we mean an explanation which is founded on the principle of causality understood as follows: "The good deed is rewarded, the evil deed is punished"; an explanation which leaves no place or very little place for any theological, mystical or superstitious agency: it is in the very nature of a good deed to produce reward; reward is automatically produced, that is independently of any exterior factor, out of the very potentiality of the good deed.

The deep reason of the origin and of the spread of this doctrine was, without doubt, a sentiment of justice. It is not just that crime should remain unpunished and virtue unrewarded. Unmerited suffering and unmerited pleasure offend us for the same reason. Hence a certitude, a sort of scientific certitude, first that sin is certain to turn into pain and a good deed into pleasure, just as for the modern physicist motion turns into heat, and, second, that pain and pleasure are respectively the product of sin and of virtue.

It may be said without exaggeration that this certitude has been, for centuries, the strongest and most popular feeling of India. Even to-day, in the castes which practise child marriage, young widows are looked upon as criminal: "What a sinner you have been to lose your husband so soon!"

With the Buddhists, the doctrine of Karman is, as a rule[1], strictly understood, and is almost everything. In the case of the non-Buddhists, with the possible exception of the 'religions of devotion' (*bhakti*), it is no less important, although it is not understood strictly[2].

We propose to examine the history of Karman, and the part of Buddhism in this history. The conclusion of this inquiry will be (1) that the Buddhists did not discover Karman, but (2) that they were among the first to give a reasonable and moral definition of Karman. Moreover the Buddhists alone were successful in drawing from the doctrine of Karman all its consequences:

[1] Nāgasena in *Milinda*, p. 134 (translation, I, 191) is not strict.

[2] See W. Hopkins, 'Modifications of the Karma Doctrine,' *J.R.A.S.*, 1906, p. 581, 1907, p. 665.

human destiny, cosmogony and theogony are, in Buddhism, built on Karman.

II

There were, at the time of Śākyamuni, (1) unbelievers, deniers of soul, transmigration and action, (2) believers in transmigration and in destiny, (3) believers in transmigration who foreshadowed the doctrine of action, (4) believers in transmigration and in action.

We have, but briefly, studied the development of philosophical analysis which, for a long time, had been destroying the old religious and cosmical notions of the Āryas. This analysis created an esoteric theology—literally a gnosis—took a pantheistic or monistic direction, and finally made prominent the idea of the universal Self.

But that is only one of the branches of the philosophical evolution, the 'orthodox' branch, or the Vedic or Brahmanic branch properly so called. In contrast with pantheists and mystics, there were materialists and positivists—many more, as it seems, in old India than later.

Our sources, which are both Brahmanic and Buddhistic, agree on the whole[1]. Brahmanic

[1] See Hastings, *E.R.E.*, art. 'Materialism.'

sources lay much stress on the impiety of the 'would-be philosophers,' 'philosophasters' (*paṇḍitamānika*) who do not believe in the Veda and in Sacrifice. Buddhists, who themselves broke with sacerdotalism and theology, are especially preoccupied with the negation of soul and future life.

The common name for the 'unbelievers' is *lokāyata*, 'mundane,' and *nāstika*, 'negator,' 'denier,' people who say: *na asti*, 'it is not'; that is, when a priest or a mendicant wants an alms: "There is nothing for you"; and also: "There is no such thing as a gift, a sacrifice, an offering, a result of good or evil deeds"; "there is no mother, no father": parents are not entitled to any respect; "no ascetic or Brahman has discovered truth or can ascertain the reality of another life": the sacerdotal tradition and the revelations of the holy men, leaders of ascetic orders, are alike falsehoods and vain pretences to extort money.

The unbelievers had probably a sort of philosophy. When we get more precise information concerning them, that is some centuries after the time of Buddha, we are told that the Nāstikas were strong materialists, in the modern meaning of the word. Man is made of material elements;

psychical phenomena are to be explained by the special possibilities of these elements when combined in a certain mixture: just as a mixture of rice and water develops an intoxicating power, in the same way consciousness arises in the living body.

However it may be with the ancient Nāstikas, the old Buddhist texts report their views as follows[1]:

> Man is composed of four elements. When Man dies, the earthy element returns and relapses into the earth; the watery element returns into the water; the fiery element returns into the fire; the windy element returns into the wind; the senses pass into space. Four men, with the corpse as a fifth, go to the cemetery, murmuring prayers. But the bones are bleached in the flame, and the offerings of the living perish in the ashes of his pyre. Wise and fool alike, when the body dissolves, are cut off, perish, do not exist any longer.

Thus spoke Ajita of the garment of hair.

Therefore, as says Purāṇa Kassapa:

> There is no guilt for the man who mutilates or causes another to mutilate, who kills, takes what is not given, breaks into houses, commits dacoity, or robbery, or adultery; and so on....Should he make all living creatures one heap, one mass of flesh, there would be no guilt.... Were he to go along the Ganges giving alms, and ordering gifts to be given...there would be no merit....

Such were the strange sermons of the unbelieving ascetics; for ascetics had an absolute

[1] *Dialogues of Buddha*, I, pp. 46, 69, 71, 73.

right of preaching the truth. As says the King Ajātaśatru: "How should such a one as I am, think of giving dissatisfaction to any ascetic or Brahman in my realm?" In India, thought was free; opinion was no crime; but evildoers were summarily dealt with.

Side by side with the thorough Nāstikas, a few philosophers, while believing in soul and transmigration, denied action and reward.

There are eighty-four hundred thousand periods during which both fools and wise alike, wandering in transmigration, will at last make an end of pain....The happiness and pain, measured out, as it were, with a measure, cannot be altered in the course of transmigration; there can be neither increase nor decrease thereof. Just as a ball of string will stretch just as far as it can unwind, just so both fools and wise alike are wandering in transmigration exactly for the allotted term.

There is no cause, either ultimate or remote, for the depravity or rectitude of beings; they become depraved or pure without reason and without cause. There is no such thing as power or energy or human strength or human vigour. Beings are bent this way or that by their fate, by their individual nature.

Nor were the Brahmans very clear concerning the power which predetermines transmigration. It is true that references to Karman are not wanting:

The spirit, at death, takes upon itself another new form, a form of Fathers or of Gandharvas, of divine or human nature, or of any other kind of being....As he acted and as he walked, so he becomes. He who does good becomes a good being, he who does bad becomes a bad being; he becomes pure by pure action, evil by evil action.

Elsewhere we meet a formula which is distinctly Buddhistic in tone and in meaning.

Man's nature depends on desire. As his desire, so is his aspiration; as his aspiration, so is the course of action which he pursues; whatever be the course of action he pursues, he passes to a corresponding state of being.

But, according to an important passage in the same book, the doctrine of Karman is a new doctrine, a doctrine to be kept secret. In the course of a philosophical tournament—such tournaments are not a rarity from the oldest times down to Akbar—Jāratkārava Ārtabhāga questions Yājñavalkya on the destiny of the dead, and the celebrated Brahman answers: "Give me your hand, my friend; we two alone must be privy to this; not a word on that subject where people are listening." And the narrator dryly summarizes the debate they had privately: "What they said, they said regarding action; by pure action, man becomes pure."

To sum up, references to Karman are not numerous in the old Brahman literature, the

Brāhmaṇas or Upaniṣads. In the view of the authors of these books, sacrifice and esoteric wisdom are much more important than Karman. But it is only natural that liturgical treatises (Brāhmaṇas) should consider sacrifice as the best means of improving future life; and, as concerns the philosophico-mystical treatises (Upaniṣads), they deal chiefly with the merging of the individual Self in the great Self; the common idea is that this great aim can be realized by the possession of a mystic wisdom; and accordingly the Upaniṣads are little concerned with the problem of action and reward. Therefore we are not justified in arguing, from the relative silence of the old texts, that the doctrine of Karman was not already widely known.

The best reason we have for believing that the doctrine of Karman was not new, but was widely known at the time of Śākyamuni, is to be found in the very teaching of Śākyamuni and in the history of the church.

Many, among the ascetics who joined the primitive brotherhood, were believers in Karman. The Jaṭilas, the 'ascetics with matted hair,' were to be admitted without the noviciate or probation of three months imposed on others, "because they believe in Karman." The Master, for this reason, made an exception to the rule which wisely secured a thorough preparation for full admission to the Order[1].

But our point is that the teaching of Śākyamuni on Karman is in no way an improvisation, and clearly obtains a success which it could not have obtained if it had been new. Śākyamuni taught a path to deliverance, because many people were anxious to get deliverance. The same holds good for Karman. Human destiny, free will, the efficacy of penance for destroying sin,—together with such questions as 'Is the soul the body?', 'Is the universe infinite?'—were the topics of lively discussions among hermits and mendicants; while the laymen, who actually fed all these troops of spiritual men, took great interest in these philosophumena and were disposed to admit the doctrine of Karman. This doctrine, as well as the doctrine of transmigration which it so happily completes, was already deeply rooted in the popular feeling.

[1] It may be urged that this exception proves that the belief in question was also exceptional. We think that the only legitimate conclusion is that no other constituted body of ascetics was acceptable as a whole to the Buddhists.

III

As far as we can surmise—there are many more conjectures than ascertained facts in this old history—Śākyamuni was the first or one of the first to give a reasonable and moral definition of Karman.

That appears from the comparison between the Buddhists and the Jains, a powerful mendicant order which originated or was reorganized a few years before Śākyamuni.

The Jains are, in many respects, very much like the Buddhists, so much like that the different origin of the two sects was for a long time denied. They are good atheists—they even object to the common Indian saying, *devo varṣati*, Ζεὺς ὕει; they believe that Karman is the governing force in human destiny.

But they cherish the most materialistic idea of Karman. They are of opinion that bodily and verbal actions are important, that they create a subtle matter that envelops the soul and produces retribution—whereas mental action is weak, inefficacious.

Buddhism, on the contrary, teaches that there is no Karman without consciousness and even premeditation.

Karman is twofold: (1) volition (*cetanā*), or mental or spiritual action (*mānasa*), and (2) what is born from volition, what is done by volition, 'what a person does after having willed,' namely bodily and verbal action[1].

By giving gold, while intending to give a stone, a gift of gold is indeed made; but, as it has not been premeditated or willed, the act is as if it were not done. It is not 'appropriated'; it is not 'stored up' (*upacita*); it will bear no fruit. In the same way, if a man kills his mother when striking at what is believed to be a pumpkin, there is no matricide, there is no murder, there is only destruction of a fruit.

The Jains criticize this doctrine strongly, and would believe that the unintentional murderer of his mother is a hideous criminal. The man who commits murder, or who harms in any way a living being, without intent, is none the less guilty, just as a man who touches fire is burned.

But this would lead to palpable absurdities. The embryo and the mother would be guilty of making each other suffer. The murdered man himself would be guilty, for he is the object and therefore the origin of the action of murder.

[1] *Saṃyutta*, II, p. 99; *Madhyamakavṛtti*, p. 306.

Further the comparison of the fire is not a happy one: a man would not be guilty of murder if he got another person to commit it, for we are not burnt when we touch fire by means of another. Again unconscious sin would be more heavy than conscious sin: a man who touches hot iron without knowing that it is hot, is likely to be more deeply burnt than the man who knows[1].

This contrast of the Buddhist doctrine with the Jain doctrine draws our attention to this fact that the views of Śākyamuni, which seem to us reasonable indeed, but rather evident, were bold and new, and of far-reaching consequences.

To take the risk of acquitting the unintentional murderer was in fact to break with the immemorial conception of sin. We do not mean that, in the oldest times, a moral conception of duty and sin did not exist; but sin was also looked upon as a sort of contagious fluid, a sort and the most dangerous sort of impurity. One becomes sinful, hateful to gods and men, not

[1] When stating these consequences of the Jain opinion, the author of the *Abhidharmakośa* (chapter IV) forgets that Nāgasena teaches Milinda the very Jain doctrine and the simile of the fire. In this connexion, compare Plato on the 'lie in the soul' (*Rep.* Bk. II, 382), and Bourdaloue on the 'fausse conscience.'

only by sinful acts, but also by kinship or any sort of contact.

A consequence of this materialistic conception is that sin is to be dispelled by physical contrivances, is to be burnt out by penances (*tapas*), by the heat penance—standing between the four penitential fires, with the sun above—when the sin is as it were 'extracted' from the body along with the perspiration. Or the sin is to be washed away by baths, especially by baths in the holy water of the Ganges.

These old and always living speculations have been somewhat spiritualized in some Indian religions, but Buddhism alone radically ignores or cancels them. We must consider this definition, "Karman is volition, and bodily or verbal action which follows volition," as one of the steps in the history of the Indian thought.

Volition is all important. Our future depends on our present volition, and our present state depends on our past volition.

> All that we are is the result of what we have thought; it is founded on our thoughts; it is made up of our thoughts. If a man speaks or acts with an evil thought, pain follows him, as the wheel follows the foot of the ox that draws the wagon.

We are what we think, we are what we will.

While emphasizing the all-importance of volition, Buddhism does not minimize the importance of bodily and verbal action, the action that a person does after having willed. To forsake the secular life and actually join the Buddhist Brotherhood is an entirely different thing from resolving to do so. To kill a man is more hideous than to resolve to kill a man. It is true that, in the case of a Rishi, endowed with magical power, the resolve to kill actually kills; but in the case of ordinary mortals murder supposes a will strong and persistent.

A point of the later scholasticism is worth mentioning. While a pure volition only leaves traces (*vāsanā*) in the series of thoughts, bodily and verbal actions—which are corporeal and material—create a thing of a particular nature, semi-material (*rūpa*) and semi-spiritual, which is called 'action,' although it is really a result of action. Scholastics name it *avijñapti*. Once produced by a voluntary verbal or bodily action (*vijñapti*), the *avijñapti* exists and develops of its own accord, without the agency of thought, whether a man is waking, sleeping or absorbed in contemplation.

The idea which gave rise to the conception of *avijñapti* is clear enough. A man who has taken the vows (*saṃvara*) of the religious life by a solemn declaration (*vijñapti*)—a verbal action—is not a man like others. He has engaged himself to avoid certain actions, killing, stealing, etc., during his life-time. He is not always pondering over this engagement during sleep or at any other time; nevertheless as long as he has not formally given up his vows or committed an action contrary to his vows, he remains a man who has taken the vows, literally 'who is restrained (*saṃvṛta*)'; his avoidance of sinful actions is another thing than the casual avoidance of sinful actions by a man who has taken no vows.

An action, to be 'complete' and really 'fruitful,' apt to 'ripen,' must consist of three parts: (1) the preparation, that is the first volition and all the contrivances necessary to the so-called 'principal action.' For instance, a butcher arises, takes some money, goes to the market, buys a goat, has the knife in his hand; (2) the principal action: the killing of the goat, the actual death-dealing blow; (3) the 'back' of the principal action: the cutting up and selling of the meat, etc.

The Buddhist theory of confession is based upon these considerations. The moral benefit or merit (*puṇya*) of a gift is totally or almost totally lost for the giver if he regrets his generosity; in the same way a sin is not done, it is only half done, if one regrets one's sin. Confession, as it is practised by the Buddhist monks, is not a sacramental rite; it is an expression of repentance, an affirmation: "I will not do it again," and also the accomplishment of one of the vows of a monk: "I will not tell lies." Confession does not destroy sin; but it is the intention of concealing sin that makes sin 'complete.'

IV

According to the Buddhists, the only action (*karman*) is volition and intentional word and deed; further action, to be complete, must be 'prepared'—not casual or impulsive—and 'backed up,' approved of afterwards, not counteracted by repentance.

It must be added that Buddhists lay all the stress on the morality of actions, and in this was a marked progress.

Morality, of course, was not unknown in ancient India; but, to say the least, the ideas were somewhat confused by ritual prejudices. In Buddhism, all the intricate fabric of the rites of purification and of sacrifice falls to the ground. Whereas it was thought that Indra, King of the gods, had obtained his sovereignty through a hundred sacrifices (hence his name, Śatakratu), Buddhists believe that sacrifice is of no avail, that sacrificial murder is a murder. Whereas austerities and purifications of many kinds were deemed necessary, Buddhists condemn them as so many superstitions (*śīlavrata*). In the same way they abandon the most pious among the pious works of yore, gifts to the dead, funeral rites: the monks took no care of the funeral of Śākyamuni himself.

Morality alone makes the value of an act.

The fact has often been emphasized that the Buddhist rule of morality is, or seems to be, a purely negative one: to avoid the ten sins. "Do not kill, do not take what is not given, do not indulge in illicit love,"—three bodily sins. "Do not use mischievous, rude, mendacious, foolish language,"—four verbal sins. "Do not cherish lust, hatred, wrong doctrines, especially the doctrine that there is annihilation at death,"—three mental sins.

A layman has to accept this tenfold discipline or restraint (*saṃvara*) to be admitted as a 'devotee' (*upāsaka*). Monks take a more strict discipline: for instance, they renounce not only illicit love, but also marriage; but the negative character of their morality (*bhikṣutā*) is the same as it is for laymen.

Are we to conclude that positive morality, altruism or love, is foreign to the Buddhist ideal of conduct? As is well known, scholars disagree.

R. Pischel, following Taine, has maintained that love of one's neighbour is the leading motive of Buddhism[1].

It may be first observed that Indian philosophers have been from of old keen enough to understand that man has always in view his own interest, even when he seems to be the most generous and disinterested. They have discovered La Rochefoucauld long ago. "It is for the sake of Self that Man loves cattle, wife, sons or riches," says the Upaniṣad. And Śākyamuni comforts the king Prasenajit and his wife the queen Mallikā ('Jessamine'); this loving pair ashamed at discovering that each of them preferred his or her Self to anybody else: "I do not see," says Śākyamuni, "any living being in the three worlds who does not prefer his own Self to anything[2]."

Self-love, self-love well understood[3], governs all the actions of a Buddhist, whether monk or layman.

The monk has arrived at a stage in the spiritual career when a purely egoist behaviour is necessary. The monk has not to practise

[1] Taine, *Nouveaux Essais*; Pischel, *Buddha*; Oldenberg, *Aus Indien und Iran*, and *Deutsche Rundschau*, 1908, VI, p. 380.

[2] *Saṃyutta*, I, p. 75.

[3] *Saṃyutta*, I, p. 71 (Warren, p. 216); *Jātaka*, III, p. 279.

good actions,—such actions he has done in heaps in former births,—he has only to avoid evil actions, to avoid any occasion of an evil action, to extinguish desire. His ideal is absence of desire, absence of action. The monk has broken natural and social bonds; he has no obligation towards his former wife, his former children[1].

The case is quite different as concerns the layman. The layman has to acquire merit, he has to do positive acts of morality, good acts. "A good act is the act that benefits one's neighbour; a bad act, the act that harms one's neighbour[2]."

Such a dogmatical definition of good and evil is scarce, and as a rule the morality of acts is to be known by their fruits: "A good act is an act that ripens into a pleasurable existence; a bad act, an act that begets suffering." Proofs are innumerable that Buddhists recommend good acts of every description. A man who does not commit any sin will be reborn as a man, not as an inhabitant of hell, an animal or a ghost; but if this sinless person is wanting in positive

[1] Oldenberg, *Buddha*, tr. Foucher[2], p. 149.

[2] The *Abhidharmakośa* states that 'wrong view' (see above, p. 46) is a sin; then it proceeds to discuss this statement: "How can it be said that 'wrong view' is a sin since a good act is the act that benefits one's neighbour...."

meritorious actions, especially in giving, he will be reborn as a poor man. Whereas a generous man, who has indulged in some sin, will, it is true, pay for this sin by rebirth in an inferior state (hell, etc.); but he will also, after being released from the ties of sin, enjoy on this earth, as a rich man, or in heaven, as a god, the fruit of his gifts.

Among meritorious actions, giving is the most fruitful. It may be interesting to state the principles of the valuation of the merit of giving.

One must take into account:

1. The qualities of the giver, faith, morality learning, and his intention in giving: 'I give in order to receive in my turn,' 'I give because I have received,' 'I give because my parents and grand-parents were wont to give....'

2. The manner of giving: with respect, with the right hand, at the opportune moment.

3. The qualities of the object given, excellence in colour, smell, and so on. There is nevertheless an episode parallel to the widow's mite.

4. The qualities of the person who receives, that is, as Indians say, the 'field' (*kṣetra*) on which the gift is poured. Much depends, in Buddhism and in Brahmanism, on the fertility of the field. Our sources distinguish (*a*) the

excellence in relation to the kind of existence: a gift to a wicked man has a hundred times the value of a gift to an animal; (*b*) the excellence due to suffering: gifts to the poor and to the sick are especially productive of fruit; (*c*) the excellence due to services received: our parents are our benefactors and have a right to our gifts; the preacher, who teaches us the Buddhist doctrine, gives us a second birth, better than the first; (*d*) last not least, the excellence due to qualities, morality, knowledge, in a word to sanctity. Buddhists are not as jealous as the Brahmans, and Śākyamuni extols the gifts made to the ascetics of the rival sects. But a Buddhist monk is evidently a better 'field' than a heretic. A gift to a Buddha, small as it may be, is very good indeed.

The gift given by a man who does not care for reward, who gives in order to free himself from greed, who understands fully the Buddhist doctrine,—that is, who knows the unsubstantiality (*nairātmya*) of the giver, of the gift and of the receiver,—that is the best gift.

The confusion of 'good' (*kuśala*) and 'meritorious,' 'bearing a pleasant fruit' (*puṇya*), which seems to be one of the consequences of the doctrine of Karman as understood by the Buddhists, leads to some results that are not perfectly sound. For instance, a man will abandon secular life in order to be reborn as a god and to enjoy pleasures incomparably greater than the pleasures of human life. The story of Nanda is a good illustration of this case: once this relative of Śākyamuni realizes that his wife cannot vie with the celestial damsels—just as the female apes cannot vie with his wife—he becomes a monk, for he will obtain, through actual continence, sensual pleasures of the highest degree[1].

An action is good when it does not aim at immediate (*aihika*) ends, when it is made in order to obtain reward in a future life; it is bad when it aims at an immediate end, viz. pleasure in this life. This rule, practically a golden rule, is possibly a little too empirical. But to appreciate it without prejudices, we must remember, first, that a system of morals is not to be estimated from the details of casuistry, and, second, that the true Buddhist is the man who does not care for merit or reward, but who strives for Nirvāṇa.

[1] Aśvaghoṣa's *Saundaranandakāvya*, partial translation by A. Baston, *J. As.* 1912, I, p. 79.

CHAPTER IV

THE DOCTRINE OF KARMAN AND TRANSMIGRATION, COSMOGONY, THEOGONY

I. Mechanism of transmigration. II. Classification of actions and mechanism of their fructification. III. Destiny, free-will, solidarity. IV. Cosmogony. V. Theogony.

I

The Buddhists did not discover the notion of Karman, but they were amongst the first to emphasize its importance, and probably the first to understand clearly its nature. It remains to be seen how the doctrine of Karman provides them with a rationalistic theory of the soul as a transmigrating non-entity, with a theory of cosmogony, or creation of the world, and of theogony, or origin of the gods.

Man, according to the Buddhists, is not a metaphysical entity, an individual, a thing in itself (*chose en soi*), a self. Were he a Self, he could not be modified; he could not be extinguished; he would endure as he is and as he was, for eternity; he would be lifeless and unconscious, since life and consciousness are succession and change. Man is a complex and impermanence itself.

But, on the other hand, Man is not lacking in unity and continuity; he is a living complex, not a haphazard succession of unconnected phenomena; he is a chain of causes and effects.

The diverse elements of this chain are to be classified under three headings: (1) passions or desires, (2) actions and (3) what is called fruit (*phala*), that is sensations together with the immediate conditions of sensation.

To be less technical. There arises a desire which may or may not be followed by an action (act of volition and physical action). If there is action, this action is to be rewarded; in Buddhist language, it ripens, it produces fruit: the fruit is pleasant or unpleasant sensation, together with the whole physical and psychical organism without which sensation is impossible. Sensation, in its turn, produces desire—love or hatred—which again produces action. The wheel continues to roll on this 'threefold rim': desire, action, ripening of action.

Such is the general principle.

Much space would be required to develop all

the consequences of this principle; but what follows is the essential.

If we consider the changes a being undergoes during the long journey through transmigration —more exactly the changes which modify the complex we call a being—it is evident that these changes are of a manifold nature. On the one hand, they are either physico-psychical or moral. On the other hand, they are either small or great, either of the nature of an evolution or of the nature of a revolution.

There is an incessant change both physico-psychical and moral.

In the course of one existence, that is, between what is called conception or birth and what is called death, physico-psychical changes are, as a rule, small. When a being is born as a man, an animal, a god, it lives and dies as a man, an animal, a god. There are exceptions. It is, for instance, recorded that a certain monk for having abused the congregation and having styled his colleagues "Women!" suddenly became a woman. It happens that the murderer of a saint is thrown down alive into hell, and, without dying as a man, is wrapped in a body of hell. Such events are rare. The physico-psychical changes that take place during a life do not, as a rule, affect the general frame of the body or the mind.

Moral changes may, on the contrary, be enormous, as is the case when a man becomes a saint or a murderer, when a man 'plants a strong root of merit' or when he commits a hellish sin. Let us observe in passing that man and woman alone are usually regarded as being capable of sin or good deeds. The other states of existence, hells and paradises, are almost exclusively states of enjoyment, of reward or punishment.

But then comes death. Death occurs when the mass of actions that were to receive retribution in some existence is exhausted. A life as a rule—for there are exceptions—is measured out with a measure, in length, in pains and pleasures, to make up exactly the quantity and the quality of reward for the enjoyment of which this life has been started. Death, we say, is the moment for great physico-psychical changes which depend on moral changes. At this moment, a sort of balance is made of the moral debit and credit. The moral status is ascertained and the next existence is to be in accordance with this status. A new physico-psychical complex suited to this next existence is to be created, and, in order to create it, the last state of consciousness, that is, the dying consciousness, takes such and such a form. For instance, if the new existence is to be hell, the dying man hears the cries of the damned; he dies and, at the same moment, the dying consciousness is continued into the first state of consciousness of a new infernal being. This first state of consciousness of a new being is what we call technically 'birth-consciousness' or 'conception-consciousness' (*pratisaṃdhivijñāna*).

Here we have to make a distinction.

Infernal beings and gods have no parents: their birth is 'apparitional,' that is, is accounted for as a magical apparition. To put it otherwise, the birth-consciousness of a new god or creature of hell is apt to make for itself and by itself, out of unorganized matter, the body it is to inhabit. Therefore the birth of such beings will follow immediately after the death of the being which is to be reborn as infernal being or god.

The case is different, as a rule, with animals, ghosts and men; with such beings, birth or conception presupposes physical circumstances that may not be realized at the moment of the death of the being to be reincarnated. Physical conditions of conception are wanting if a being is to be reborn as a dog at a moment when the season of dogs is over. Physical conditions of birth are wanting for such animals as maggots, which are born from putrid meat, if there is no meat to be found in such a state. In these cases, and in many similar cases, the dying consciousness cannot be continued at once into the birth-consciousness of a new being.

Hence a difficulty which is clearly solved by the schools which maintain the so-called 'intermediary existence' (*antarābhava*). According to these schools, the dying consciousness is continued into a short-lived being, named *Gandharva*, which lasts for seven days or for seven times seven days—evidently a notion borrowed from the animistic theories of old. This Gandharva, very like a disincarnated spirit, creates, with the help of the conceptional elements, an animal embryo, a ghostly or human embryo, as soon as it can find opportunity. It is driven by the wind of acts towards the right matrix; but there are, sometimes, mistakes: for instance it happens that the new animal is born as a jackal instead of a dog.

The decisive element on which depends the

next existence is the dying consciousness. It is the dying consciousness which originates the birth-consciousness, and which is the immediate cause of the birth-consciousness.

That the moral dispositions at death are of great importance has been admitted by many a religion, in India and outside India. And that these dispositions depend on the life which is ending, that a man dies as he has lived, this is also a common notion and not a bad piece of psychology.

Ideas that have been cherished during life reappear at death; a man has, in this crucial moment, a vivid memory of his sins and good deeds,—and, in the latter case, of the reward for which he has been striving.

Śākyamuni says this in so many words: A man, who is endowed with merit, has been thinking: "May I, when my body dissolves, obtain rebirth in a powerful princely family!" He thinks this thought, dwells on this thought, cherishes this thought, and this thought, which he has thus cherished and fostered, will be his last thought. "This is, O monks, the avenue and path which leads to rebirth in a powerful princely family."

The last thought is often a summary and the

result of the moral and intellectual life of a dying man. But such is not always the case.

The last thought is to bring about the next existence; it is therefore predetermined by the action which is to be rewarded in this next existence—and this action may be a very ancient action, performed many centuries ago. This will be made evident by an example.

When an animal is to be reborn as a man, it will have a dying consciousness to this effect. This dying consciousness does not depend on any action or thought of the animal, for animals are dull and incapable of morality; this dying consciousness depends on some ancient good deed which was to ripen into a human birth and which, for a long time, has been prevented from producing its result: there was a mass of bad actions first requiring retribution. Now that this mass of bad actions has borne its fruit—let us say a score of infernal or animal rebirths—the turn of the good action comes at last, and the last animal in the score of animal rebirths cherishes in its last moment the ideas, desires or images, which will cause a human rebirth.

The Buddhists say that if the seed of a plant has been dyed a certain colour, this colour will reappear in the flower although it does not exist in any of the stages of development of the plant, in the stem and so on. A western comparison is better and really to the point: heredity. A man may be like his grandfather, not like his father. The germs of a disease have been introduced into the organism of an ancestor; for some generations they remain dormant; they suddenly manifest themselves in actual disease. So intricate is the living complex; so mysterious the laws of heredity, we should say; so mysterious the reward of actions, say the Buddhists.

We believe that this comparison is to the point. For every moment in the life of these physico-psychical complexes which are called living beings, is the heir of the preceding one, and carries all the potentialities of a very long past.

II

A few remarks are necessary on the time of the reward of actions.

There are actions which are styled *lokottara*, supermundane, actions that are not born from desire. They bear no fruit, except the fruit of deliverance (*visaṃyoga*); they destroy desire; they cancel the reward of the other actions;

they lead to Nirvāṇa; they are part of, or rather they constitute the path to Nirvāṇa. We shall study them presently[1]. We are now concerned with the actions which foster transmigration, that is produce rebirth or reward: because they originate from desire.

Some are necessarily rewarded, some are not.

I. The first are to be classified in three groups: acts rewarded in the present life; acts rewarded in the next existence; acts rewarded later.

1. When compared with the reward in another life, the reward in this life is looked upon as small. Pain in this life is nothing when compared with pain in hell; human pleasures cannot vie with celestial pleasures.

An important point is that the retribution of a sin depends to a large extent on the moral status of the sinner.

When a man is deficient in merit, a slight evil deed will ripen into an infernal existence. A good man, on the contrary, will expiate the same evil deed in this life: a slight punishment, although, says the text, it may appear not slight but very painful.

It is as if a man were to put a lump of salt into a small cup of water: the water would be made salt and undrinkable. But if the same lump of salt were put into the river Ganges, the water of the Ganges would not be perceptibly modified[2].

[1] See below, p. 153. [2] *Aṅguttara*, I, 249 (Warren, p. 218).

In the same way, the moral status of a good man is not modified by a small sin; but this sin, if complete, is to be rewarded; it is therefore rewarded here below.

2. Some acts are necessarily rewarded in the next existence. Their retribution cannot be delayed by the retribution of any other act; and they are accordingly styled 'immediate,' *ānantarya*. Parricide, for instance. Such sins prevent the acquisition of Sanctity.

3. There is a third category of sins, which, heavy as they may be, are not necessarily rewarded in the following existence. Their retribution may be delayed to make room for the retribution of other acts; in that case they are rewarded 'later on.' Or, and this point is interesting, as they do not prevent the acquisition of Sanctity, it happens that they are turned into actions to be rewarded here below.

The classical illustration of this rule is the case of Aṅgulimāla, "the man with a garland of fingers," a celebrated robber and murderer. Śākyamuni converted him, owing to some ancient root of merit he possessed hidden under a heap of sins. Aṅgulimāla became a monk and a Saint, that is a man who has obtained deliverance and will not be reborn; but he did not avoid the fruit of his sinful actions: when he goes into the town to collect alms, as the monks do every day, the populace greets him with stones; he is covered with blood; his begging bowl is broken and his robe torn. In this state he comes to Śākyamuni who says to him: "The reward of your evil deeds, you should have experienced for long years, for many thousands of years in hell; and you are now experiencing it already in this life[1]."

II. A few words will give an idea of the actions which are not necessarily rewarded, which may be abandoned or 'left behind.' A Saint, who has acquired much merit, is not obliged to enjoy this merit in paradise: he will, at death, reach Nirvāṇa. Again, a man who is to be reborn in one of the highest heavens and to obtain Nirvāṇa there—in technical language an Anāgāmin—abandons all the actions, good or evil, that were to be rewarded in hell, here below or in the inferior paradises. In the same way, say the texts, a man who changes his residence for ever, leaves his debts behind him.

We are now able to understand the mechanism of the fructification of actions[2].

[1] *Majjhima*, II, p. 97. The story of Losakatissa (*Jātaka*, I, p. 235, tr. I, p. 110) is interesting in this connexion. See also Vajracchedikā, § 16.

[2] *Abhidharmakośa*, chap. IV.

Existences are good or bad: human and divine existences are good; infernal existence, ghostly existence, animal existence are bad.

An existence, a rebirth, is caused, technically 'projected' (*ākṣipta*), by a single act. All men are reborn as men owing to a good action: how is it then that so many men are unhappy? Because a number of acts combine to condition an existence; hence the variety of the living beings belonging to the same kind.

A man, owing to wrong views or bad inherited dispositions commits one of the ten sins: he commits murder, theft, adultery; he uses mendacious, malignant, rude, foolish language; he nourishes covetous designs, hateful sentiments, wrong views. These sins are supposed to be complete, that is, fully premeditated, consciously done, cherished and approved: they are to be necessarily rewarded in the following existence; and accordingly the man is reborn in hell. When the sin is very heavy (owing to repetition, etc.) this man dies in some hell only to be reborn in another hell; and that ten times, a hundred times, a thousand times. His infernal existences and his sufferings are what is technically called the 'fruit of ripening' (*vipākaphala*) of his sin.

The birth-projecting force of the sin is not

yet exhausted; but it is diminished. Therefore, we have now animal rebirths, one, ten, or a hundred animal rebirths. The sufferings undergone in these animal existences are again the 'fruit of ripening'; but the nature of the animal is a fruit called *niṣyandaphala*, a 'fruit similar to the action.' For instance a murderer will be reborn as a tiger; a thief as a cunning animal, a serpent, and so on.

The birth-projecting force of the sin is now exhausted; accordingly, there is room for the projecting power of some ancient good act which was 'to be rewarded later'; and now this act projects a human life: this human life, together with the pleasures to be enjoyed in this life, is the 'fruit of ripening' of the good act.

But these pleasures will be few and small. Such a human existence will not be a happy one. The former inhabitant of hell, the former animal, although reborn as a man, remains under the influence of his ancient sin. He suffers pains akin to this sin. An ancient murderer will be short-lived, he will be crushed to death; a thief will be poor; an adulterer will have an unfaithful wife, and so on. These pains are a part of the *niṣyandaphala* of the ancient sin. The second part consists in mental or moral dispositions in accordance with the dispositions which, long ago, culminated in an actual sin. The murderer, after a long abode in hell (*vipākaphala*), has been reborn as a tiger (*niṣyandaphala*) and, suffered as a tiger (*vipākaphala*). Dying as a tiger, he is reborn as a man (*vipākaphala* of a former good act), but as a man destined to violent death and of a cruel nature (*niṣyandaphala* of the sin). And so on. In short, Karman explains everything that concerns 'the world of living beings' (*sattvaloka*), inhabitants of hell, animals, ghosts, men and gods; the power of gods and kings, the physical beauty of women, the splendid tail of peacocks, the moral dispositions of every one.

III

Ancient India, as does also to a large extent the India of to-day, believed in destiny, a τυχή, the *daiva*, from *deva*, god (also *vidhi* or *haṭha*), a blind power against which human wisdom and endeavour are weak. Man is not even free to be prudent and wise, *deus quos vult perdere prius dementat*, a formula which could be the motto of many an episode in the Mahābhārata.

Buddhism does not deny the power of

destiny; but it maintains that destiny is only one's own former action. A man is born from his own deeds, not from his parents, or more exactly he has the parents he merits to have:

> My action is my possession; my action is my inheritance; my action is the matrix which bears me; my action is the race to which I belong; my action is my refuge[1].

As it is said:

> All that we are is the result of what we have thought and done.

But the question is whether "all that we do now, in this present life, is the result of what we have done"? The conception of destiny left some room for free-will: does the doctrine of Karman, understood strictly as the Buddhists are prompt to understand it, leave any loophole?

Here we are, as is often the case with Buddhism, in the very middle of a jungle of contradictions.

On the one hand, Buddhist ontology does not admit the existence of an agent, a doer (*kartar*):

> No doer is there, naught save the deed is found.

There is no Self, but only a 'series' of physico-psychical phenomena. We have seen that a volition is only the further state of a desire.

[1] *Majjhima*, III, p. 203; *Milinda*, I, p. 101.

On the other hand, we are told that our actual dispositions are inherited. A man is not cruel or covetous because he chooses to be so, but because he has just been a tiger or a lustful animal.

Further, living beings are without real connexion one with another. They are water-tight series of thoughts. Each of them eats the fruit of his own actions. Accordingly Śākyamuni teaches that "Nobody can harm or benefit another," for "The Self is the protector of the Self: what other protector could the Self have?" The most powerful demon cannot harm a man who has not merited to be crushed by him; and, inversely, Buddha himself cannot favour a disciple with a lesson which this disciple has not merited to receive.

The problem of free-will is a difficult one, but it can be said that Buddhism has added difficulties and contradictions of its own to a problem in itself difficult. These difficulties are the more striking in Buddhism, because Buddhism, which flatly denies freedom and solidarity, is essentially a discipline of endeavour and benevolence.

Buddhist philosophers, it is true, do not

hide these difficulties, but they do nothing to explain them away.

There is no self, no doer, no free agent: *kartā svatantro nāsti*; there is only a succession of psychical states. Every Buddhist knows quite well this essential truth: not only in the scholastical texts but even in the common language, the word *saṃtāna* or *saṃtati*, 'series,' is used for what we call a soul: "At this time the series which is now named Śākyamuni was called Sunetra." "When the Scripture says that consciousness (*vijñāna*) is to take up its abode in the matrix, the meaning is [not that a conscious Self is reincarnated, but] that a series of states of consciousness continues to develop in the embryo."

The Buddhist authors are always aware that the soul is only a series. This does not prevent them from preaching endeavour as the only means of salvation, and, without paying any attention to verbal contradictions, they say: "The series is to be drawn against the flow of passions by means of good acts, owing to a strong endeavour; the series must be driven away from pleasurable objects." They do not explain how an unsubstantial series of thoughts can draw itself against passions and prejudices which are the series itself.

Just as the Christian philosophers—Calvin or the Jansenists—who strictly limit or are inclined to deny human free-will, are nevertheless fairly good 'teachers of energy,' in the same way Buddhists lay all the stress of their teaching on the cultivation of endeavour, on self-restraint (*saṃyama*, *saṃvara*[1]). The virtue of energy (*vīrya*) is indispensable, for the struggle is hard against lust, hate, and error. Śākyamuni was an 'enlightened one,' *buddha*; but he was equally a hero, a conqueror, *vīra*, *jina*; and his disciples must be worthy of such a king.

A most happy contradiction indeed.

A second contradiction is no less striking and happy.

Buddha is not a saviour. "Buddha is only a preacher; the path to deliverance is open to everybody; but, according to their dispositions, some will be delivered, some will not." Again, the very fact that we are reborn as men, in Jambudvīpa, in India, at the time when Buddha opens the Path, is the result of our own good deeds accumulated during many ages of men. But Buddha looks twice every day in all directions in order to see whether he can help some of his fellow creatures; owing to his 'eye of a

[1] Mrs Rhys Davids, *Psychology* (1914), p. 37.

Buddha,' he is keen to perceive any 'root of merit' which any miserable and wretched man can have stored up at any time in the past; he takes any trouble to bring this 'root of merit' to maturity by appropriate sermons or miracles. Owing to his strength of benevolence, he converts whomsoever he will. His disciples are urged to imitate, in some way, the virtues and the peaceful conquests of the Master. They have to practise the best sort of gift, the gift of the Doctrine (*dharmadāna*); they have to convert and edify sinners by friendship and benevolence.

To sum up, the doctrine of Karman is the root of morality. It makes clear the necessity of "avoiding what is evil, practising what is good, purifying one's thought"; and "that is," in short, "the rule of Buddha." The idea that our enemies are only the delegates of our old sins will make us patient and compassionate: "My enemies do harm to themselves when they try to harm me; and they do not harm me, nay they are very useful to me." But there are certain consequences of the doctrine of Karman. What is to be said about denial of free-will, impossibility of benevolent action? Buddhists see and plainly state these consequences, for they are candid men and good scholars. But they do not trouble themselves about them; they write and they live as if they had not seen them.

In that they are wise, and they only follow the golden principle of Śākyamuni. It happened one day that, being questioned on the doctrine of Karman, he soberly answered: "My teaching is to do good deeds, to avoid evil deeds." And, more than once, he ventured to say that this doctrine is inconceivable or incomprehensible (*acintya*), that is to a human mind, for a Buddha is omniscient.

IV

The variety of the material universe (*bhājanaloka*), including the hells, the earth with the plants, and the heavens, depends upon some cause.

To admit that things are such as they are, because they are such as they are, that lotuses are lotuses, thorns thorns, owing to their own nature (*svabhāva*), such is the doctrine of the philosophers 'who attribute the origin of all things to chance' ('fortuitous-originists[1]').

That is pure nonsense. The truth is that actions bear a 'fruit of mastery' (*adhipatiphala*),

[1] *Dialogues of the Buddha*, I, pp. 41, 71.

that is, they create or organize the material things necessary to their reward.

A being is to be reborn as a god—the Sun god for instance—of such a size, of such a physical beauty and strength, destined to live so many ages of men. All these advantages are the 'fruit of ripening' of the good deeds of this being. But this god must have an abode, a celestial palace—the moving chariot, fifty miles in diameter that we call the Sun: this palace is the 'fruit of mastery.'

In the same way, at the beginning of a cosmic period, the whole material universe is created by the 'mastering' energy of the mass of the ancient acts that are to be enjoyed by its future inhabitants. The 'receptacle world' (*bhājanaloka*) is the 'fruit of mastery' of the mass of the acts of the 'world of living beings' (*sattvaloka*).

V

Another aspect of Karman, Karman as a theogonic power, has never been emphasized in Brahmanism as it is in Buddhism.

The Brahmans sometimes venture to think that the gods are not eternal or immortal. The gods have reached a divine status by their pious doings, their sacrifices, their penances—not necessarily by 'good' actions. It is well known that many gods are bad, fond of killing, stealing, wantonly destroying, and that Śākyamuni did his best to tame them. The gods die when their reserve of divinity is exhausted by the very experience of divine pleasures: they are the happy or rather unhappy possessors of a 'peau de chagrin' and, as the hero of Balzac, they know that it is drawing in.

Further the Brahman gods have to struggle for life, for their divine life. While they are enjoying their reserve of power, there are in the vast world ascetics who are heaping up penances and merits, penances and merits which can be, at the will of the ascetics, turned into divinity at the cost of the actual gods. The gods defend themselves as they can. The Epic (*Mahābhārata*) contains numerous stories of temptations, when the gods, anxious about the accumulating austerity of some Muni, dispatch to him heavenly damsels to disturb his pious exercises. A dangerous employ: Śakuntalā, the most charming child of Indian fancy, was born in such circumstances; but Menakā, her mother, perished. Śākyamuni himself was attacked by the daughters of Māra, the god of love and death.

But this theogony in terms of merit, penance, or sacrifice, is, in Brahmanism, only a theoretical view and a literary topic. It does not endanger the traditional mythology or jeopardize the status of the supreme god, whether Brahmā or Viṣṇu or Śiva,—so many names for the Absolute.

In Buddhism, Karman and transmigration apply, in fact as in theory, to all beings.

The position of the gods, when compared with the Buddhist saints, is a subordinate one. It is true that the actions resulting in the present happiness and power of the gods are good actions; but these actions were accomplished through 'worldly' motives: the gods have reached the reward for which they have been striving: *vani vanam*. A monk who has begun his career towards a loftier aim, Nirvāṇa, is by far superior to the gods, even in magic.

As concerns Brahmā, who according to the Brahmans is Īśvara, the Lord, the universal sovereign who cares for everything, who takes account of actions and governs the transmigration of individual beings, who designs the successive creations of the universe after the successive periods of chaos—the Buddhists do not recognize him. They know that an infinite number of gods, each with the title of Brahmā, but having a separate name of his own, have reigned in succession, each during a cosmic period (*kalpa*). Such gods are great gods; they enjoy the fruit of very good deeds, the fruit of very high meditations tinged with altruism[1]; they are quasi spiritual, non-sexual gods, but by no means sovereigns of the world, creators, or overrulers of the retribution of actions.

When, at the beginning of a cosmic period[2], after the chaos, the inferior part of the universe is to be rebuilt, the heaven or palace of Brahmā is the first part of the 'receptacle world' to appear, as the 'fruit of mastery' of the actions of the being who is to be the Brahmā of the period. Then this Brahmā is produced in this palace. As he does not remember his former existences, he is apt to believe that he is born from himself, that he is self-existent (*svayaṃbhū*). After a time, he gets tired of his solitude; he thinks that servants and companions would be pleasant, and, at the same moment, there are produced the gods Companions of Brahmā; that is to say, owing to the special nature of their own acts, certain beings are born in the Brahmā's palace. Brahmā, of course, believes that he has created them, and they, in turn, believe that they have been created by Brahmā. They

[1] Mrs Rhys Davids, *Psychology* (1914), p. 103.

[2] See art. 'Cosmology' in Hastings, *E.R.E.*

adore Brahmā, and this religion of Brahmā has been propagated among men.

This is brought out in the following story[1]:

There was a monk indulging, against the teaching of the Master, in cosmological inquiries. In order to know where the world ends, he began journeying far away in the sky, interrogating in succession the gods of the successive heavens. The gods 'Servants of the Four Kings of the cardinal regions,' said to him: "Ask the Four Kings"; the Four Kings said to him: "Ask the Thirty Three Gods."...The monk finally arrived in the heaven of the Servants of Brahmā: "We, monk," said they, "do not know where the world ends. But there is Brahmā, the Great Brahmā, the supreme one, the mighty one, the all seeing one, the ruler, the lord of all, the controller, the creator, the chief of all, appointing to each his place, the ancient of days, the father of all that are and are to be. He will know that."—"Where then is that Great Brahmā now?" asked the monk.—"We, monk, know not where Brahmā is, nor why Brahmā is, nor whence." "But," added the gods, "he may suddenly appear." And, before long, Brahmā indeed became manifest, and the monk asked him where the world ends. Brahmā answered: "I am the Great Brahmā...the father of all that are and are to be." —"I do not ask you, friend," said the monk, "as to whether you are indeed all that you now say. But I ask you where the four great elements—earth, water, fire and wind—cease, leaving no trace behind." Then the Great Brahmā took that monk by the arm, led him aside, and said: "These gods, my servants, hold me to be such that there is nothing I cannot see, understand, realize. Therefore I gave no answer in their presence. But I do not know where the world ends....Go you now,

[1] *Dialogues of the Buddha*, I, p. 280.

return to the Lord, ask him the question, and accept the answer according as he shall make reply." The monk returned to Śākyamuni who told him: "Long ago, O monk, sea-faring traders were wont, when they were setting sail on an ocean voyage, to take with them a land-sighting bird....Such a bird would fly to the East, and to the South..., and if no land were visible, it would come back to the ship. Just so, O monk, do you, having sought an answer to this question, even up to the world of Brahmā, come back to me."

Śākyamuni is the only source of truth. It happened that the god Indra met some monks, and wondered at the wisdom of their sayings: "Here is," he said, "a fine doctrine. Did you discover it by yourselves?" The monks answered: "When there are to be seen, in the neighbourhood of a large granary, men bearing corn, some in baskets, some in their robes, some in their hands, it is not difficult to guess where the corn comes from. In the same way, every 'good and true saying' (*subhāṣita*) comes from the Lord[1]."

[1] *Aṅguttara*, IV, p. 163. See below, p. 153.

CHAPTER V

NIRVĀṆA

I. Introductory. Pessimism and deliverance or Nirvāṇa. Difficulties in ascertaining the nature of deliverance. II. Etymology and meaning of the word Nirvāṇa. Three opinions on the state of a Saint after death. III. Annihilation. IV. 'Unqualified deliverance.' V. Conclusion. Scholastic views on the conflicting statements in the Scriptures.

I

Older Buddhism, more accurately the Buddhism of the old Books, is almost exclusively a discipline of deliverance, deliverance from rebirth and death, deliverance from transmigration. Like the other disciplines of deliverance, the doctrine of the Upaniṣads or the Sāṃkhya, it is founded on pessimism.

Indian or Buddhist pessimism is often looked upon as a natural consequence of the belief in transmigration. Much has been written on this subject—sometimes perhaps 'unintelligently,' as E, J. Thomas rather strongly asserts[1]. India

[1] *Buddhist Scriptures*, p. 20.

as a whole has never been, as it were, hallucinated by the idea of rebirth and death. Common religious people dreamt of paradises, of eternal paradises; and there has been, from the beginning, side by side with the Buddhist discipline of salvation, a Buddhist religion, a moralized Hinduism. The doctrine of transmigration itself opens out cheerful possibilities: rebirth does not necessarily mean rebirth as a creature of hell, as an animal, a ghost, a miserable man. The Śatapathabrāhmaṇa expressly states that rebirth in this world is a reward. The so-called 'bad states' (*durgati*) are not without their own satisfactions: to be a serpent or a ghost 'endowed with a great magical power' is after all not despicable. But the most striking evidence that transmigration did not frighten the Buddhist monks is that they have built a number of heavens, fit for any temperament: enjoyable and meditative heavens. They know, better than the Brahmans themselves do, the path that leads to the heaven of Brahmā! In a word, Transmigration is death again and again, but it is also inexhaustible life.

But there were in the days of Śākyamuni many men to whom the very idea of death proved intolerable. Why, owing to what climatic, racial, social circumstances it is so, is and will remain a mystery. But the fact is beyond doubt, and it is well illustrated by the importance given, in the old Buddhist Literature, to this simple statement, which looks like a great discovery: "Life indeed ends in death[1]."

Śākyamuni teaches that the ocean is not large and deep enough to contain the tears which through millions of existences fill the eyes of one man; he comforts a mother who had just burnt on the funeral pyre her daughter ironically named Jīvā, Life, by telling her that she had already burnt, thousands of times, in the same burning place, the same daughter.

There is no happiness in life:

> Then I asked them: "Can you maintain that you yourselves for a whole night, or for a whole day, or even for half a night or day, have been perfectly happy?" And they answered "No."

Buddhists go so far as to deny that *suṣupti*, the profound sleep praised in the Upaniṣads, is free from suffering; they would refuse to the Great King the few hours of rest which the Socrates of the Apologia is willing to concede to him.

[1] It may be remarked in passing that this sentence seemed to the first translators to be really too simple, and, through a wrong separation of the words, they turned it into: "Life indeed is death" (*Dhp.* 148; *Saṃ.* 1, p. 97).

Then I said to them: "Do you know a way, or a method, by which you can realize a state that is altogether happy?" And still to that question, they answered "No[1]."

In a word, there were many, men and women, old and young, noblemen and outcasts, merchants and robbers, who had learnt to despise the trivial joys of existence, who wished for absolute happiness and despaired of reaching it. Deliverance from rebirth seemed to them a goal for which it was worth while to strive.

Deliverance, or Nirvāṇa, is the central idea of the teaching of Śākyamuni and the *raison d'être* of the religious life:

"As the vast ocean, O monks, is impregnated with one flavour, the flavour of salt, so also, O monks, this my Law and Discipline is impregnated with but one flavour, with the flavour of deliverance[2]."

It seems therefore that we should be amply provided with definitions of Nirvāṇa and that there should be no doubt as to the actual meaning of this word.

As a matter of fact, we know what Nirvāṇa

[1] *Dialogues of the Buddha*, I, p. 287.

[2] *Cullavagga*, IX, I, 4.

is as well as the Buddhists themselves, and it is not our fault if we are not able to give an unambiguous statement. The Buddhists were satisfied with descriptions which do not satisfy us.

On the one hand, whereas we have been for centuries trained to make our ideas clear, this was not the case with Indians. The historian has not to deal with Latin notions worked out by sober and clear-sighted thinkers, but with Indian 'philosophumena' concocted by the ascetics whom we shall describe presently: men exhausted by a severe diet and often stupefied by the practice of ecstasy. Indians do not make a clear distinction between facts and ideas, between ideas and words; they have never clearly recognized the principle of contradiction.

Buddhist dialectic has a four-branched dilemma: Nirvāṇa is existence, or non-existence, or both existence and non-existence, or neither existence nor non-existence. We are helpless.

We are prepared to admit that there may be degrees in 'being,' pleroma and kenosis. But our logical categories are not numerous enough for a theory of degrees in 'voidness' or non-existence as Mātṛceṭa states it:

Others than Buddha have won the same liberation or Nirvāṇa, but in Buddha the superiority is altogether great. All the liberated are void, but this leaves room for the superiority of Buddha: the void of a pore of the skin compares but poorly with the large void of the sky[1].

Moreover, we look at the Buddhist doctrines from the outside. Whereas Nirvāṇa is for us —*pace* the neo-Buddhists—a mere object of archæological interest, it is for Buddhists of paramount practical importance. Our task is to study what Nirvāṇa may be; the task of a Buddhist is to reach Nirvāṇa.

Comparisons are misleading; but the *Imitatio Christi* may be quoted: "What avails the understanding of the holy Trinity, if we displease the Trinity?" We have to please God, not to realize the nature of God. Rather in the same way, Śākyamuni prohibited discussion concerning Nirvāṇa. For a Buddhist, the important thing is, not to know what Nirvāṇa is, but to reach Nirvāṇa; and inquiry concerning Nirvāṇa may prove disastrous. As historical students, our only danger is to make mistakes, and we can afford it.

[1] *Varṇanārhavarṇana*, 1, 10–11, ed. F. W. Thomas, *Indian Antiquary*, 1905, p. 145, and Hoernle's *Manuscript Remains*, 1, p. 78.

II

The primitive meaning of this celebrated word, Nirvāṇa, seems to be twofold: on the one hand, 'becoming cool, cooling'; on the other hand, 'blowing out,' 'extinguishing.' There is a *nirvāṇa* of a man who is thirsty as well as of a candle[1].

Hence two directions in the evolution of the religious or philosophical meaning of the word. Cooling, refreshment, the refreshment of a man who is suffering, the cooling of a man who is hot with desire, comfort, peace, serenity, bliss. Also extinction, detachment or extinction of the fire of the passions, negative bliss or extinction of suffering, annihilation or extinction of individual existence.

Each metaphor is apt to convey two distinct ideas.

On the one hand, Nirvāṇa is Sanctity (*arhattva*). For a Saint (*arhat*) has become cold (*śītībhūta*), as he is no more burned by the fire of passions, and he has extinguished this fire.

On the other hand, Nirvāṇa is the ultimate end of a man, the state of a Saint after death.

[1] See art. 'Nirvāṇa,' in Hastings, *E.R.E.*

For Nirvāna may be cooling of suffering—an eternal refreshment—or extinction of existence.

In the Pāli literature, it is not always evident whether the word Nirvāṇa (*nibbāna*), with its numerous synonyms, means Sanctity, the state of a living Saint, or the state of a Saint after death. The first meaning is the more common. On the other hand, in the Sanskrit literature of Buddhism, Nirvāṇa generally means the state of a Saint after death. We will use the word Nirvāṇa in this last meaning and style Sanctity the state of a living Saint.

Two points are beyond doubt:

1. Nirvāṇa is the *summum bonum.*
2. Nirvāṇa belongs to Saints and to Saints alone.

Let us consider the death of an ordinary man and the death of a Saint. Men who at death are endowed with desire and who have not destroyed their ancient Karman, have to be reborn according to their merit and demerit. They continue transmigrating. A Saint has not to be reborn; he has passed beyond birth, old age and death; in the technical phrase: "He has destroyed rebirth; he has led the religious life; he has done what he had to do; he has nothing more to do with life here[1]."

So much is certain.

But it can be maintained either (1) that the dead Saint is annihilated, cut off, does not exist any longer; or (2) that he has reached an immortal state; or (3) that we can only assert, without being able to state positively what deliverance is, that he is delivered from transmigration.

In other words, Nirvāṇa is either annihilation, or immortality, or 'unqualified deliverance,' a deliverance of which we have no right to predicate anything.

It is fairly certain that, from the beginning, there have been Buddhists who held one of these three opinions. The point is to realize the relative importance of these conflicting views, and to state which is the prevailing teaching of the Scriptures and the ruling idea of the Buddhist religious life.

[1] There are, in the Pāli scriptures, two formulas. The first one, which we believe is the earlier, is translated above, *nāparam itthatāya*; it points out that the Saint is not to be reborn in this world. The second one, *n'atthi tassa punabbhavo*, states that the Saint is not to be reborn. In the Sanskrit canon, the first formula is worded as follows: *nāparam asmād bhavāt prajānāmi*; also a clear and definite negation of rebirth.

III

That Nirvāṇa is annihilation results—at least for us—both from the general principles of Buddhist philosophy and from clear statements.

There is nothing permanent in Man. Man is a complex of bodily and spiritual constituents which form a physico-psychical organism. In the case of men who are not Saints, this organism is not cut off at death when the body perishes, because, owing to desire and to Karman, it is continued in a new organism, heir of the first. Now suppose that—as is the case of a dying Saint—desire is destroyed and Karman to be experienced (*vedanīya*) absent, there is no cause for rebirth. There will not be a new complex of bodily and spiritual constituents to be reborn when a Saint dies. And there is no existence possible outside these constituents: the Buddhist criticism has sedulously destroyed all the mystical or psychological *data*—idea of a transcendent soul (Sāṃkhya), idea of an immanent absolute (Upaniṣads, Vedānta)—that could give any support to a conception of survival of whatever kind. Selflessness precludes all possibility of survival.

Moreover it is certain that the Buddhists—I mean the Buddhists who compiled the Scriptures

—were well aware of this consequence of the dogma of Selflessness. When the question is discussed of the survival of the Saint, the answer is often—often, not always—in the terms we have just stated: "Any matter or body (*rūpa*) which could be said to be the matter or the body of the Saint no longer exists," and so on with the immaterial (*arūpin*) constituents of the human organism: "Any cognition whatever which could be said to be a cognition of the Saint no longer exists." Elsewhere: "Henceforth, when I shall be asked whether a Saint perishes at death or not, I shall answer: Body is perishable[1]."

It cannot be said that there is a chariot where there is neither pole, nor axle, nor any of the constituent parts of the chariot. In the same way, there is no Saint where there are not the elements which constitute this pseudo-individuality called a Saint[2].

It may therefore be safely maintained that Nirvāṇa is annihilation.

[1] *Saṃyutta*, IV, 374, and elsewhere.

[2] The Yamaka dialogue (*Saṃyutta*, III, p. 109, see the translation of Warren, p. 138, of Oldenberg, tr. Foucher[2], p. 279) is not, as Oldenberg believes, an evidence against the doctrine of annihilation. On the contrary *Udāna*, VIII, 3 (*Itivuttaka*, § 43), which Oldenberg understands in the meaning of annihilation, is by no means clear.

Does that imply that Buddhists aim at annihilation? Not exactly so. Scholars who have maintained that Nirvāṇa was chiefly looked upon as annihilation do not say that a monk leads the religious life in order to be annihilated at death, but that he leads the religious life in order to become a Saint. Sanctity is the goal. Sanctity is the *summum bonum*, deliverance, Nirvāṇa.

In the words of Rhys Davids[1], the deliverance Śākyamuni preaches is "a salvation from the sorrows of life, which has to be reached here on earth in a changed state of mind." The hope of a monk is to obtain "a lasting state of happiness and peace to be reached here on earth by the extinction of the fire of lust, hatred and delusion." 'A lasting state of happiness...' from the moment when Sanctity is attained to the hour of death. Buddhism would thus be only a discipline of happy life here below.

Our opinion is that these statements are very wide of the mark. But it is only fair to admit that much may be said in their favour and that they are to some extent exact. We must honestly admit that Sanctity—coupled with annihilation

[1] *Manual* (1877), pp. 110–115; *Hibbert Lectures* (1881), pp. 161, 253; compare Childers (1875), p. 208.

—may have been and has been, for many a monk, the ruling motive of the religious life.

According to the philosophical tenets of Buddhism—strictly understood—on the one hand, transmigration is pain; on the other hand, the Saint, at death, does not exist any longer. The life after death having lost any interest for the Buddhist, he had only to work out a supreme ideal of happiness in this very life. That he did. It is a professional happiness. The monks, technicians of Sanctity—that is, absolute detachment, mental and moral apathy—were apt to make Sanctity the chief point of a discipline of their own. *Ils n'étaient pas Hindous pour rien.*

India has always been full of awe and admiration for the ascetics and ecstatics who have reached a thorough tranquillity, a perfect ἀταραξία, insensible to pleasure and to pain and therefore altogether happy. Such men were a natural product of the Indian soil. They have been the pattern of Brahman and Buddhist Sanctity.

The Brahmans have worked out a metaphysical interpretation of the ecstatic Saint. They style him a *jīvanmukta*, 'delivered yet living,' and assert that he is actually identified with Brahman, that is to say with the immanent Absolute.

The Buddhists have as a starting point the same type of Saint; but they do not attempt any metaphysical interpretation. They are satisfied with a study of the psychological ascertained facts. To put it shortly, the Buddhist Saint is plunged in the concentration 'where notion and feeling are destroyed.'

While dwelling in concentration, the Saint is happy. When he, sometimes, opens his eyes to the spectacle of the world, he is also happy. He contemplates from the shores of the island of serenity the painful agitations of men: he is free, they are fettered by desire. He enjoys one of the most delicate pleasures in this life, the pleasure of self-complacence coupled with altruism. He says, in the style of the Lucretian sage:

> The wise, climbing the terraced heights of wisdom looks down upon the fools; serene he looks upon the toiling crowd, as one who stands on a mountain looks down upon those that stand upon the plain[1].

A sublime pattern of this serene happiness was afforded by Śākyamuni. A halo of mystery is not wanting. Neophytes long for such a happiness, for such a perfection. To become like Śākyamuni is no mean ideal.

[1] *Dhammapada*, 28.

It may be urged that Sanctity being its own reward and ending in annihilation is not a cheerful prospect.

But scholars who identify Nirvāṇa with annihilation would say:

1. Annihilation is the end of the misery of life, and Buddhists are pessimists, Buddhists are sick of existence[1].

2. Indian philosophers, as a rule, do not attach much importance to the survival of personal consciousness, which is for us a necessary characteristic of survival, or rather is the survival itself. With the strict Vedāntists, Nirvāṇa (*brahmanirvāṇa*) is the end of the illusion of individuality; with the Sāṃkhyas, Nirvāṇa is the eternal isolation (*kaivalya*) of the soul, eternal unconsciousness. Therefore, when a Buddhist admits that Nirvāṇa is annihilation, he only goes a step further.

Again a man works out his ideal of happiness after death from the pattern of his ideal of happiness here below. According to the Buddhist and Indian standard, the supreme happiness for a living man is to reach and to dwell in the

[1] Milton's lines are not Buddhistic:

> For who would lose, though full of pain, this being,
> These thoughts that wander through eternity?

concentration 'where feeling and notion are destroyed.' As a matter of fact, annihilation (*uccheda*, *nirodha*) is this happy state of concentration continued for eternity. Therefore annihilation is a state and a happy state.

3. Nevertheless Indian ascetics were men; and men long for immortality, not immortal death, but immortal life. There was however a means, an excellent means of gratifying the needs of the heart while maintaining the dogma of annihilation.

Death has nothing awful for young people, who have the whole of life before them, who do not realize that "Life indeed ends in death." In the same way, annihilation in Nirvāṇa will be easily accepted if Nirvāṇa is 'postponed.'

The monk may be given some existences to reach Nirvāṇa.

At the beginning, almost all the disciples of Śākyamuni became Saints, to be extinguished at death: but soon a new theory was framed according to which the state of a Saint requires more than a life-long exercise and, therefore, is to be realized by steps. There are disciples on the road to Sanctity to whom seven or less numerous new existences, human or celestial, are allowed to complete their sanctification.

It is worthy of notice that Brahmanism has built parallel theories of gradual salvation. Side by side with the 'merging in Brahman during this life'—the only notion known in the earliest texts—the Vedāntists instituted a discipline leading to deliverance by steps (*kramamukti*).

The reasons of this new departure were certainly manifold. One was that Sanctity came to be looked upon as a difficult task. The other, and possibly the stronger, was that monks were really happy to postpone Nirvāṇa. A 'half saint' is sure to reach Nirvāṇa at the end and sure to enjoy pleasant rebirths on the way. His lot is a lucky lot indeed.

Neo-Buddhism—Mahāyāna—went far in this direction. Nirvāṇa was relegated to a remote distance. According to the Lotus of the True Law, a man, to reach Nirvāṇa, has to become first a Buddha, and, to become a Buddha, thousands and thousands of strenuous and charitable lives are necessary. In this way, Buddhism succeeded in getting rid, if not of the very notion of Nirvāṇa, at least of Nirvāṇa as a practical ideal. The starting point of this change is to be found in the old theory of the steps to Sanctity.

IV

The preceding remarks have done full justice to the views of Childers, Rhys Davids, Pischel and other scholars. But we do not believe that the definition they have given of the aim of the Buddhist religious life, viz. Sanctity coupled with annihilation, conveys *the* right idea of Nirvāṇa.

It is true that, according to the doctrinal tenets, *strictly* understood, a Saint is annihilated at death. It is true that there are categorical statements to this effect, and Max Müller was wrong in denying that Nirvāṇa in the sense of annihilation is a dogma of Buddhism. It is a dogma of Buddhism. But Buddhism is not an orthodoxy, a coherent system of dogmas; it is rather a practical discipline, a training; and in this discipline, the notion 'Nirvāṇa-annihilation' is chiefly a result of philosophical inquiry and, therefore, a notion of secondary rank.

This notion was not an 'original purpose' of Buddhism, a doctrine aimed at by Śākyamuni. Śākyamuni did not start with such a notion of the deliverance from birth, old age, death and suffering; this notion was forced upon him—or upon the Church—because he had been rash enough to deny the existence of a Self and to invent—or to adopt—the theory of a composite soul.

This fact must be emphasized, for it seems to be important both for the history of Buddhism and the history of religion in general. Logic or dialectic is a dangerous auxiliary of religious thought: doctrines may be altogether reversed by the development of some dogma; certain premisses being accepted, conclusions will be as inevitable as destiny itself. But, when such conclusions are out of harmony with the general spirit of the doctrine, with the average temperament of the faithful, with common sense, either they fail to obtain general acceptance and beget only heresies and sects, or they remain mere theoretical and 'bookish' views, pure ideas, without becoming what the philosophers style 'idées-forces.'

We have seen that the extreme consequence of the doctrine of Karman, "What we do is the result of what we have done," has not been admitted by the Buddhists, firm maintainers of Free-will despite their ontology, their psychology and their ethics. Many another instance, Indian or European, might be quoted. (1) The conception of Being in the Upaniṣads and Vedānta logically ends in pure Monism (*advaita*); and Śaṃkara in fact is a pure monist, or tries to be a pure monist. But there are many Vedāntist schools which maintain a variety of 'qualified monisms' (*viśiṣṭādvaita*). (2) The notions of predestination or absence of Free-will are easily, we do not say logically, developed from the dogma of God, creator and all-powerful. These notions found in Mahomedanism a favourable ground: they agree with the uncompromising and austere monotheism of Islam and with what is called 'oriental apathy.' While, in Christendom, they have been repeatedly developed only to be repeatedly checked.

In the same way, or rather, somewhat in the

same way, final annihilation was in Buddhism only a corollary of the denial of a Self, a result, not an object aimed at by Śākyamuni, not a postulate of the Indian mind, depressed as it may have been by the miseries of life, intoxicated as it may have been by philosophical meditations.

In fact, there are evidences that would lead us to believe that Śākyamuni did his best to avoid this result, and even objected to a definite statement of such a result.

These evidences are to be found in a number of texts which profess to state the position taken by Śākyamuni as concerns metaphysics, as concerns the existence of a soul (*jīva*) distinct from the body, as concerns the survival of a Saint. This position is a sort of agnosticism or pragmatism.

Śākyamuni knows everything, but there are truths he refuses to reveal. The reason of his silence is that the knowledge of the truths which are not necessary to Sanctity is a dangerous knowledge; or that a man, and even a Saint, is not intelligent enough to grasp certain truths.

That Śākyamuni knows everything, no Buddhist has ever doubted. One of the most celebrated titles of a Buddha is *sarvajña*, 'omniscient,' or with more precision, *sarvākārajña*, 'who knows everything as it is.' Buddhists believe that Śākyamuni, when he obtained *bodhi*, illumination or enlightenment, acquired universal knowledge. He does not know, at any moment, everything, because his knowledge, like all knowledge, consists of so many distinct and successive acts of attention (*manasikāra*), but he knows everything he desires to know. Śākyamuni, therefore, never says: "I do not know," but in some circumstances he says plainly: "You will not know, you shall not know."

Here is a simile[1]:

> Śākyamuni was staying at Kauśambī in the grove of Aśoka trees. He took a few Aśoka leaves in his hand and said to his disciples: "What do you think, O monks, whether these few leaves, which I have gathered in my hand, are more, or the other leaves yonder in the grove?"—"The few leaves which the Lord holds in his hand are not many, but many more are those leaves in the grove."—"So also, O monks, is that much more which I have learned and not told you than that which I have told you."

Śākyamuni is said to have left unsettled, to have set aside and rejected the questions concerning the existence of a soul (*jīva*) distinct from the body, and the nature of Nirvāṇa.

[1] *Saṃyutta*, v, p. 437; compare *Milinda*, p. 413; *Dīgha*, II p. 100.

As a matter of fact, there are in the Canon many sayings of Śākyamuni which, at least indirectly, settle these questions in the sense of soullessness and annihilation. We may admit (1) that some disciples, or many disciples, felt dissatisfied with the nihilistic doctrines, and therefore hoped, at the bottom of their hearts, that they misunderstood the Master. Let us not forget that the disciples of Śākyamuni came to him as to the discoverer of the path to immortality (*amṛta*). Or, possibly (2) there were monks without any prejudices, anxious only to be made quite sure about Nirvāṇa, not by logical conclusions drawn from psychological premisses, not by metaphorical and conflicting phrases, but by a direct and definite statement from the lips of the Omniscient. Last, not least, (3) there were monks who had never heard of the nihilistic sayings of Śākyamuni and wondered at Śākyamuni's silence concerning soul and survival.

Māluṅkyāputta was one of these monks[1].

"There are," said Māluṅkyāputta, "questions that Buddha has left unsettled, has set aside and rejected... whether the soul and the body are identical; whether the soul is one thing and the body another; whether a saint exists after death; whether a saint does not exist after death; whether a saint both exists and does

[1] *Majjhima*, 1, 426; Hastings, *E.R.E.* art. 'Agnosticism.'

not exist after death; whether a saint neither exists nor does not exist after death....The fact that Buddha does not settle these questions does not please me. I will inquire. If he does not answer, in that case I abandon the religious life under the rule of Buddha."

Māluṅkyāputta questions Buddha accordingly, and ends by uttering very strong words: "If the Lord does not know, the only upright thing for one who does not know, is to say: I do not know."

Buddha, of course, does not confess that he does not know, nor does he answer the questions.

Did I ever say to you: "Come, lead the religious life under me and I will explain to you these points"? or did you say to me: "I will lead the religious life under you on condition that you will explain to me these points"?

Māluṅkyāputta confesses that Buddha has not given any pledge to that effect, and that he himself did not state any condition of his accepting the Buddhist rule. And Buddha continues:

Any one who should say: "I will not lead the religious life under Buddha until Buddha explains all these points," that man would die before Buddha had ever explained these points to him.

Men are suffering from actual pains which are to be healed at once; they are poisoned with desire, and desire prepares for them new rebirths and new sufferings: desire is to be crushed.

It is as if a man had been wounded by an arrow thickly smeared with poison, and this man were to say: "I will not have this arrow taken out until I have learnt whether the man who wounded me belongs to the caste of the warriors...before I have been told his name, his clan, his stature, his complexion; before I have been told the nature of the bow, of the bow-string..." This man would die before he knew.

As the knowledge of all these circumstances has nothing to do with the removal of the deadly arrow, even so the knowledge of the metaphysical points is totally extraneous to the discipline which abolishes suffering and desire, to the discipline of Sanctity:

The religious life does not depend on the dogma that the soul and the body are identical, on the dogma that the soul is one thing and the body another thing, on the dogma that a saint exists, does not exist, both exists and does not exist, neither exists nor does not exist after death. Whether this or that dogma is true, there still remain birth, old age, death, for the extinction of which I am giving instructions....What I have left unsettled, let that remain unsettled.

Thus spoke Śākyamuni.

These 'agnostic' statements are astonishingly to the point. Whatever opinion a Buddhist may entertain concerning the destiny of a dead Saint, this opinion is an obstacle to serenity, to detachment, to Sanctity, and therefore to Nirvāṇa itself.

If Nirvāṇa be a happy state, the monk would strive for Nirvāṇa as one would strive for a paradise, and he would accordingly miss it: he would reach at death some paradise, an enjoyable but transitory paradise. If Nirvāṇa be annihilation, Nirvāṇa would again inspire desire or abhorrence: in both cases, Sanctity is impossible. Anxiety and speculation concerning the life after death (*antagrāhaparāmarśa*) is one of the five heresies. Therefore, "let that remain unsettled that has not been settled by Śākyamuni." A monk will reach Sanctity and Nirvāṇa, without knowing what Nirvāṇa is, and for this very reason that, owing to this ignorance, he remains free from the desire of existence (*bhavatṛṣṇā*), free from the desire of non-existence (*vibhavatṛṣṇā*): "I do not long for life; I do not long for death."

We believe that the most exact and the most authoritative definition of Nirvāṇa is not annihilation, but 'unqualified deliverance,' a deliverance of which we have no right to predicate anything.

The idea of Nirvāṇa generally cherished by the Buddhists is not a positive one. They know that existence is suffering. And they think that there is an exit, a Nirvāṇa, deliverance from transmigration, from birth, disease, old age and death; and that is indeed enough.

Nirvāṇa is looked upon as a deliverance: just as a man who is in gaol wants only to be free, even so Man does not want to be happy; he only wants to be delivered from the miseries of life. That is pessimism.

It is not absolute nihilism, nihilism boldly looked at in the face. It is a negative attitude, which does not appeal to the most innate needs of our mind; but it is also to some extent an expectant attitude, which leaves some food to the needs of the human heart. The monk strives for unqualified deliverance; he does not inquire whether deliverance is destruction or a mysterious kind of existence; but he knows that Śākyamuni is omniscient and compassionate, and such a 'caravan-leader' is the great man upon whom it is safe to rely.

V

It remains to draw the conclusion of our inquiry, that is, to strike a sort of balance between the contradictory statements with which we are confronted, and to reconcile these statements if possible.

According to the doctrinal tenets of Buddhism, accurately and profusely explained in every part of the Scriptures, Nirvāṇa is annihilation: selflessness is, from our point of view, incompatible with any kind of survival of the Saint. But do the Buddhists draw from their tenets the logical conclusion concerning Nirvāṇa? They do; or some of them do: there are categorical statements to prove that the compilers of some parts of the Scriptures identified Nirvāṇa with annihilation.

Moreover it is not doubtful that Sanctity was for many a monk the very deliverance, the very Nirvāṇa preached by Buddha.

But this conception of Sanctity as a goal in itself, if it agrees with the nihilistic view of Nirvāṇa,—Nirvāṇa in the sense of annihilation, —agrees as well with the 'agnostic' texts, with Nirvāṇa in the sense of 'unqualified deliverance.'

The whole Suttanipāta testifies to the Buddhist dislike of 'opinion.' The religious life, as depicted in this book, one of the oldest, is not compatible with any opinion. Everything supports our surmise that 'annihilation' is the result of the philosophical inquiry, a mere scholastic corollary.

Moreover, while we are not willing to 'maximize' the importance of the few scriptural texts which affirm the existence of a Self, under the name of *pudgala* (an individual, a person), these texts cannot be ignored altogether. They are old; they are no less authentic than the selflessness texts; they are the authoritative texts of the Sammitīya sect, an important school. The maintainers of the *pudgala* theory will admit that Nirvāṇa, the state of a Saint after death, is existence.

And, in this connexion, we are not sure that all the scriptural passages, which describe Nirvāṇa as a happy and stable condition, refer to Nirvāṇa in the sense of Sanctity; some of them at least may refer to the state of a Saint after death. If they all refer to Sanctity, as is often contended by scholars, the reference is more than once very obscure.

The obvious conclusion is that the ancient Buddhist tradition was not clear on the nature of Nirvāṇa as well as on many other points.

This conclusion does not please those scholars who are prepared to turn primitive Buddhism into an orthodoxy. While we believe that the scriptural contradictions—Nirvāṇa annihilation, Nirvāṇa immortality, Nirvāṇa a prohibited problem—are to be accepted as they are; while we believe that the true Buddhist state of mind is a happy syncretism, scholars of a more orthodox or less catholic temperament make a choice among the conflicting views; they deny, expressly or tacitly, the authenticity or the authority of the texts which support the view they have rejected[1].

Much is to be learned from the position taken by the philosophers of the Mahāyāna school (neo-Buddhism). They are both honest and clear-sighted; they are plainly conscious of the contradictions of the Scriptures; they are, on the other hand, firm believers in the authenticity of these Scriptures; they cannot, therefore, resort to the Gordian method of exegesis.

As *philosophers*, they have to make a choice and unanimously maintain the nihilistic interpretation of Self and of Nirvāṇa. But, as *historians*, they confess that Śākyamuni sometimes indulged in 'ontological' statements, sometimes simply prohibited inquiry concerning the 'unsettled questions,' sometimes taught annihilation. They explain why he did so, and the

[1] It is much safer to credit Śākyamuni and the primitive Brotherhood with all our texts, than to deny the antiquity of any idea to be found in these texts. "Il n'y a point," says La Bruyère, "d'ouvrage si accompli qui ne fondît tout entier au milieu de la critique, si son auteur voulait en croire tous les censeurs qui ôtent chacun l'endroit qui leur plaît le moins." Sainte-Beuve used to compare Homer in the hands of Wolf and Dugas-Montbel to the man with two lovers: "l'une arrache les cheveux noirs, l'autre les gris, et le voilà chauve."

reasons they give for the contradictions of the Master are of far-reaching importance as concerns the *philosophical* solution of the problem itself.

It is an old opinion among the Buddhists that Śākyamuni has modified his teaching according to the needs of his hearers, according to their intellectual and moral possibilities. Let us understand his position. A Buddha is a physician, the physician of this mortal disease that is named desire. Desire originates rebirth, suffering, death. In order to cure this disease, Śākyamuni had to employ 'allopathic' contrivances. He teaches that there is not a Self—and with such an emphasis that he sometimes gives the impression of being a 'materialist'—because a man who believes in the reality and permanence of his Self will love his Self, will hate the Self of his neighbour, will be anxious about the state of his Self after death, in a word will desire. He teaches that there is rebirth, because the idea of annihilation at death is likely to produce the heresy of "Let us live happily so long as we are alive." He emphasizes the happiness of deliverance, in order to induce men to give up the trivial hopes of transitory paradises and many foolish devices to this end: deliverance is better than any conceivable state of existence. Last, not least, Śākyamuni does not hide this fact that deliverance is absolute silence and annihilation, the end of suffering, because it is the end of feeling. Why does he teach such a doctrine? I dare say, because the most pragmatist of the philosophers cannot help sometimes describing things as he believes they are: deliverance *is* annihilation—and there are some few disciples worthy to be told the truth.

The simile of the physician is a Buddhist metaphor. There is another to the same effect, more Indian and also very exact. A Buddha is a tiger or rather a tigress. This tigress has to transport her cub, and accordingly takes it into her mouth; she holds it between her double set of teeth. But for the teeth, the cub would fall; but if the teeth were to be tightly closed, it would be crushed. In the same way a Buddha saves beings, transports them across the ocean of transmigration, by the parallel teaching of permanence and impermanence, Self and Selflessness, bliss of Nirvāṇa and annihilation in Nirvāṇa. Permanence, Self, bliss of Nirvāṇa: so many falsehoods. Useful falsehoods: but for them one would give up the religious training towards deliverance. Impermanence, selflessness, annihilation: so many truths. Dangerous truths, like a serpent with a jewel in its hood: it requires a clever hand to take the jewel. In the same way, few men are able to avoid being crushed by these sublime and terrible truths. Selflessness wrongly understood would lead to the wrong view that there is no survival; the doctrine of annihilation in Nirvāṇa would originate despair or distrust.

Therefore Śākyamuni has been obscure on these points, and did not avoid some contradictions; and, when an inquirer was bold enough to ask for a plain answer, he plainly answered: "You shall not know." *Cela ne vous regarde pas.*

Buddhism ends in an act of faith. Śākyamuni will lead us to salvation provided we close our eyes and follow blindly his ordinances. The important thing in Buddhism is not dogma, but practice, not the goal, the mysterious and unascertainable Nirvāṇa, but the Path, Sanctity.

CHAPTER VI

THE PATH TO NIRVĀṆA

I. The Path is the eradication of desire. II. A middle way between asceticism and indulgence. III. A threefold training in the Buddhist Truths. IV. A skilful practice of trances. V. Conclusion.

I

Nirvāṇa is the cessation of rebirth. Desire, with action consequent upon desire, is the cause of rebirth. The path leading to deliverance from rebirth must therefore be a path leading to deliverance from desire. In order to avoid rebirth, it is necessary and sufficient to eradicate desire, desire for pleasure, desire for existence, desire for non-existence or hatred of existence; that is to become a Saint, an Arhat, free from sorrow, hope, and fear.

On this point as on many another, we find in Brahmanism parallel conceptions to the Buddhist doctrine. The Upaniṣads state that Man is reborn in conformity with his desire, his aspiration, his conduct (see above, p. 64); but what is the destiny of a man who is free from desire?

"When desire ceases, the mortal becomes immortal; he attains Brahman on earth. He who is without desire, who is free from desire, who desires only his own Self which is identical with the universal Self, he obtains the accomplishment of his desire in the possession of his Self. He is the universal Self and goes into the universal Self."

It is not probable that the primitive Buddhists ever heard of these theories: the Self (*ātman*) which they know and reject is the individual Self and they never mention the Nirvāṇa of the individual Self in the great Self. But their doctrine of the Path may be shortly described as a secularisation of the Upaniṣad teaching: to free oneself from desire, while ignoring the universal Self and denying the human Self.

On the other hand, the Buddhist path is a 'rationalisation' of a number of practices which were common at this time among ascetics of every faith and aspiration.

There were many 'ford-makers,' but Śākyamuni alone has discovered the true 'ford,' or rather has re-discovered it, for the Buddhas of old had discovered it long ago; and he has designed a pattern of 'religious life' (*brahmacarya*) which is, has been, and will be, the only means to deliverance.

To give a faithful and complete image of 'the religious life under the rule of Buddha' would be a long affair. Every detail of the monastic institution, every detail of the intellectual and moral training of the monks, ought to be mentioned. Further, in order to appreciate the historical interest of these manifold data, references ought to be made to the rules of the contemporaneous sects and especially to the Brahman institutions. The very word we translate 'religious life,' *brahmacarya*, meant originally 'life of a young Brahman in the house of his preceptor before his initiation and marriage[1].'

But it will not be difficult to state the general principles of the Buddhist Path. We have only, in the words of the Sanskrit poet, to make a string on which to thread the jewels already pierced by others.

The Path is (1) a middle way between asceticism and laxity, (2) a training in the Buddhist truths, (3) a skilful practice of trances or ecstasies.

[1] Evidences for the meaning 'continence' are old; for instance *Śatapathabrāhmaṇa*, xi, 3, 3.—*Paramatthajotikā*, ii, i, p. 43.

II

Laxity or indulgence means secular married life. Asceticism means, not only, as usually with us, not indulging in morally allowed desire, but inflicting pain, penance.

The origins of asceticism,—in Sanskrit *tapas*, a word that means heat,—go far back into the past[1]. In historic India, asceticism has been turned into a religious and moral institution—a self-torture to please the deity, to wash away the sins one has consciously or unconsciously committed, to avoid sin by mortifying the flesh. While assuming these new aspects, or, to put it more uncompromisingly, while developing in a moral direction, *tapas* remained and remains an essentially magical affair. In the ritualistic books, it comes to the foreground of speculation as a creative power: Prajāpati, the Lord of the generations, performed penance, became hot and produced the worlds by the power of heat or penance. Prajāpati was a great 'penitent'; ascetics, men who practise the most extravagant penances, just as the modern fakirs, are 'penitents'

[1] On *tapas*, see Oldenberg, *Religion du Véda*, tr. V. Henry, p. 345 f. The oldest source on the ecstatic penitent Muni is Rigveda x, 136.—See Hastings, *E.R.E.* art. 'Religious Orders.'

of a smaller size, but nevertheless demiurges in their own guise, autonomous and irrepressible forces, frightful to the gods themselves.

The notion of holiness and wisdom was hopelessly confused with the notion of penance: when the idea of deliverance was discovered, men naturally thought that penitents only could have some chance of reaching deliverance.

Accordingly when Gautama, the young prince of the Śākya race, abandoned his home to secure his salvation, he first followed the common track and lived for a time—for many years—as a Muni, that is as a solitary penitent: hence his name Śākyamuni. He indulged in the most severe abstinence from food, remaining upright and motionless, hoping for a sudden illumination of mind. Five ascetics were his companions in these austerities. A Greek sculptor, five or six centuries later, produced a realistic and spiritualized representation of his emaciated body, which is one of the masterpieces of Gandhāra art[1]. But the illumination did not come, and Śākyamuni felt very weak indeed: he understood that illumination requires strength of mind; he took some food and soon reached the goal for which he had long endeavoured in vain; he became

[1] Senart, 'Notes d'Épigraphie,' III, Pl. 2 (*J. As.* 1890).

a Buddha. Intellectual achievements depend on intellectual efforts.

At the moment when Śākyamuni broke his fast, the five ascetics had deserted him, and when Śākyamuni after becoming a Buddha approached them again, they jeered saying: "Here is the one that failed in his austerities." Śākyamuni told them that he had obtained complete enlightenment. "But," they asked, "if you could not succeed in obtaining enlightenment by asceticism, how can we admit that you have succeeded when you live in abundance, when you have given up exertion?" To which Śākyamuni replied that he had not given up exertion—for penance is not the only exertion—and that his life was not a life of abundance; for the path of the men 'who have given up the world' to obtain deliverance is a middle path between the two extremes, asceticism and indulgence. "What are the two extremes? A life addicted to sensual pleasures: this is base, sensual, vulgar, ignoble, pernicious; and a life addicted to mortification: this is painful, ignoble and pernicious[1]."

[1] *Mahāvagga*, I, 6, 10 foll. (*S.B.E.* XIII, p. 93, E. J. Thomas, *Buddhist Scriptures*, p. 40). Comp. *Milinda*, II, p. 60. The history of the first days of Buddhahood is to be read in full. It bears every mark of authenticity; but we must beware that Indians are wonderful story-tellers.

While many ascetics, the Jains for instance, regarded penance as the chief element of spiritual progress[1], Śākyamuni depreciates and even, in some cases, forbids penance. (1) If penance is practised in order to obtain worldly advantages, rebirth in heaven or magical powers, the divine eye, etc., it is a purely mundane affair; born from desire, it produces desire, and is far from leading to salvation. (2) As concerns salvation, penance by itself is of no avail. To hold the contrary is 'heresy,' technically the *śīlavrata-parāmarśa*, 'believing in the efficiency of rites and ascetic practices.'

Śākyamuni does not condemn every penance, far from that. But he thinks that, even when practised by the 'orthodox,' penance presents many drawbacks.

One of them is that it is likely to beget spiritual pride, one of the pitfalls of the monks:

"Whosoever is pure and knows that he is pure, and finds pleasure in knowing that he is pure, becomes impure and dies with an impure thought. Whosoever is impure and knows that he is impure, and makes effort to become pure, dies with a pure thought."

Again some penances—abstinence from food,

[1] The *Aitareyabrāhmaṇa*, vii, 13, is strong against penance.

for instance, not to mention mutilations—are injurious to body and therefore to mind. Now full strength of mind is necessary to the understanding of the philosophical truths that are really to purify the thought. The body, therefore, must be treated without hatred if without love; the monks have to take care of their body, but it is unjust to say that they love it. As Nāgasena told the king Milinda[1]:

"Have you ever at any time been hit in battle by an arrow?"—"Yes, I have."—"And was the wound anointed with ointment, smeared with oil and bandaged with a strip of fine cloth?"—"Yes, it was."—"Did you love your wound?"—"No."—"In exactly the same way, the ascetics do not love their bodies; but, without being attached to them, they take care of their bodies in order to advance in the religious life."

But, if the body is not to be crushed, the desires of the body are to be crushed. Śākyamuni condemns every indulgence; the smallest concession may be disastrous; desire is everywhere, for we are living desire[2]:

All things, O monks, are on fire. The eye is on fire, visible forms are on fire, visual cognitions are on fire, impressions received by the eye are on fire, and whatever sensations, pleasant, unpleasant or indifferent, originate in dependence on impressions received by the

[1] *Milinda*, p. 73 (Warren, p. 423).
[2] *Mahāvagga*, 1, 21.

eye, these also are on fire. And with what are these on fire? With the fire of lust, with the fire of hatred, with the fire of infatuation.

Ear and sounds, nose and smells, tongue and taste, body—that is the organ of touch—and tangible qualities, mind and ideas are also on fire.

The right means to extinguish this fire is not the surgical method—neither vow of silence, in order to avoid sins and desires of the voice: for if that be the case, mute animals would be Saints; nor absence of thought; nor craziness, real or simulated folly (*unmattaka*), nor other stupid and stupefying devices, such as living as a cow or a dog, nor mutilations and self-torture, nor suicide, this *ultima ratio* of the Jain ascetics. Suicide is clearly an action commanded by desire or by disgust: one commits suicide to be better elsewhere or to avoid pain[1]. The Buddhist must wait his time, without longing for life, without longing for death.

The right means to extinguish the fire is the intellectual method which we shall outline presently, coupled with a moderate asceticism.

1. There were, in the primitive Brotherhood, men of penitential tendencies,—former adherents of penitential orders, for instance Mahākāśyapa

[1] Warren, p. 437.

and his followers, who had realized the superiority of Śākyamuni's teaching, who had recognized in Śākyamuni the Omniscient One and the leader of spiritual life. Śākyamuni did not provide for them a new rule: he condemned the most morbid exaggerations of asceticism and the indecent practices, nakedness and so on; but he permitted a number of mortifications (*dhūtaguṇa*) which were not in themselves objectionable.

The 'hermits' (*āraṇyaka*), the 'men of cemeteries' (*śmāśānika*) form, throughout the history of the church, a special class of monks, dangerously like the non-Buddhist ascetics. They were holy men, ecstatics and poets[1], but in some respects they were 'heretics' as well[2].

2. The conception of the truly Buddhist religious life is to be found in the Vinaya which contains the rules established by Śākyamuni and the first generation of Elders for the monks and the nuns of common observance. The more we study the Vinaya[3], the more we wonder at the common sense that is visible in the general principles and in many details.

The monks of common observance have been

[1] The 'Psalms of the Brethren' and the 'Psalms of the Sisters' (tr. by Mrs Rhys Davids) are mostly the work of 'penitents.'

[2] See my *Bouddhisme* (Paris, 1909), p. 356 foll.

[3] *S.B.E.* vol. XIII, XVII, XX.

by far the most numerous and the most important in the history of Buddhism. Absolute continence, no private property; a very strict régime which affords little or no scope for concupiscence or for individual fancy, which seems very favourable to moral mortification while avoiding any corporeal pain; the life of a wandering mendicant during the dry season, and, during rains, a cenobitic life with all the mutual concessions and admonitions this life implies. On the whole an aristocratic form of asceticism, very much resembling the asceticism of the Brahmans.

But Brahmans and Buddhists diverge on one point which is very important[1].

The Brahmans are strong on the *mos majorum*. They say: "Win only the knowledge of the Self and leave alone everything else[2]"; but they nevertheless continue to sacrifice to the gods, because the gods exist κατὰ δόξαν. They believe that every sensible man has to try to obtain eternal deliverance, and that a meditative, semi-penitential life is necessary in order to reach this lofty aim. But they cannot admit that it

[1] Beside the point we mention here, there are several others equally worthy of notice: the attitude of Buddhism and Brahmanism towards women, towards outcasts and low castes, etc.

[2] *Muṇḍaka*, II, 2, 5 (Barth, *Religions*, p. 81).

can be right to forsake the duties of caste; and, like their Āryan ancestors, they cling to the theory of the four debts. Man pays his debt to the gods by sacrifice, to the Veda by study, to the dead by the birth of a son, to men by hospitality. When he has paid this fourfold debt, then only may the Brahman abandon everything and take up his abode in the forest in order to meditate, to save himself, to die as a holy man.

As usual, the Brahmanic point of view is forcibly expressed in the Mahābhārata. We are told that an anchorite, who had 'left the world' before marrying, came to a terrible place, which was in fact the pit of hell. There he recognized his father, his grandfather, the long series of all his ancestors, suspended one below another on the open mouth of the abyss. The rope which prevented them from falling was slowly and surely being gnawed by a mouse, a figure of Time. And so many voices, some well known, reminding him of accents heard when a child, some unknown yet appealing to a profound and hidden instinct, so many voices cried: "Save us! save us!" The only hope of welfare for the long series of the ancestors is the son to be born of their descendant. The anchorite understood the lesson, married, and was able to save himself without remorse, having saved his ancestors. (See *Paramatthajotikā*, II, I, p. 317.)

The Buddhists are more consistent. Laymen, however faithful, generous and virtuous they may be, even if they practise the fortnightly abstinence and continence of the Upavāsa, cannot reach Nirvāṇa. The only Buddhist, in the proper meaning of the word, is the monk who has broken all the ties of society; and the sooner one becomes a monk, the better. Why delay in getting rid of occasions of greed and of carnal desire? Therefore children are admitted, not to religious vows, but to the apprenticeship of the vows, when they are seven years old and big enough to drive away the rooks.

If by chance, and despite the theory, a layman obtains Sanctity, he is miraculously turned into a monk; he suddenly appears shaved, garbed in the yellow robe, alms bowl in hand, like, in all his demeanour, to a monk who has fifty years of profession.

III

The moderate asceticism[1] we have described is not, to speak exactly, a part of the Path leading to the eradication of desire; it is rather only a preparation to the Path: getting away from the occasions of desire. The Path is essentially a training in the Buddhist truths.

Desire depends on the organs of sense and the exterior objects. Whereas we are not allowed to destroy the organs, since suicide, mutilations,

[1] Technically *prātimokṣasaṃvara*.

fasting are objectionable, the pleasant exterior objects are too many to be suppressed. In the same way, it is impossible to avoid every occasion of anger; solitary life does not realize perfect loneliness; suffering, disgust and anger follow the monk even in the 'empty room' (*śūnyāgāra*) where he sits to meditate.

It is said[1]:

> There is not leather enough to cover the surface of the earth in order to make it smooth. But put on shoes, and the whole earth will be smooth.

In order—not to avoid lust (*rāga*) and anger or disgust (*dveṣa*), a mere palliative—but to eradicate them, the only method is to cure one's self, to eradicate the delusion (*moha*) that originates lust and anger. We exert no mastery over Nature or over the body, but we can master our own mind and destroy the four mistakes (*viparyāsa*): looking at what really is unpleasant, impure, transitory, and unsubstantial, as if it were pleasant, pure, permanent, and substantial. We must learn to see things as they really are; technically, we must possess the Four Truths: every existence is a state of suffering or turns to suffering; existence originates in desire; cessation of rebirth—Nirvāṇa—is perfect bliss; the way

[1] *Bodhicaryāvatāra*, v, 13; L. D. Barnett, *Path of Light*.

thither is cessation of desire. First and last, we must realize the true nature of this intricate, deceiving, and most dear compound that men style 'I.'

The possession of the Truths brings about a complete renovation of the mind[1]. Desire cannot germinate in a mind which is enlightened by true wisdom, as a plant cannot germinate in salt. The agreeable and the disagreeable exist only because we believe them to be lovable or hateful: they are creations of the mind. Pain disappears as soon as we cease thinking 'I' and 'mine.' It is said:

> In the same way as a man resents the bad conduct of his wife while he still loves her, and no longer; even so the pain of the body is no longer resented when a man ceases to consider the body his own.

The possession of the Truths depends on three conditions, Faith (*śraddhā*), Sight (*darśana*), Cultivation (*bhāvanā*).

1. Śākyamuni alone has discovered the Truths; there is no hope of salvation for a man who does not take refuge in the Buddha and in the Truths revealed by him[2].

[1] The actions concerned with the possession of the Truths form this kind of Karman which destroys Karman (see above, p. 89).

[2] See my *Bouddhisme* (Paris, 1909), pp. 130 foll.; above, p. 106.

In some cases, it is possible to ascertain that the Buddha's word is trustworthy; in others, one must say: "I admit that because I believe in Buddha's word"; "Buddha knows and I do not know." The general principle is as follows[1]: "One must meditate on and understand the points of doctrine that are intelligible to an ordinary man. For the others, one must willingly admit them, saying: That belongs to Buddha's domain of vision." It is said[2]:

> When Buddha, this lion of men, roars his lion's roar in the assemblies, if anybody ventures to say that Buddha does not possess superhuman virtues, that he does not know the absolute truth, that his teaching is made up of dialectic, is accompanied by research, experience, individual intuition,—if a man ventures to think or to speak in this way and does not regret his thought or his word, he will be precipitated into hell.

2. But faith is not sufficient. Truths accepted on the authority of others do not really belong to us; they remain, as it were, extraneous and precarious possessions; they are not turned into our flesh and blood, *en sang et nourriture*. The Buddhist truths are to be understood and realized; the Saint is the man who has become,

[1] *Bodhisattvabhūmi*, 1, xviii; Comp. *Sūtrālaṃkāra*, i, 12.
[2] *Majjhima*, 1, p. 71.

like Śākyamuni himself, but under the guidance of Śākyamuni, an 'enlightened' one.

Texts which recommend or rather enjoin personal inquiry and criticism compare in strength and number with the texts which praise faith. Śākyamuni does not demand a blind adhesion; he does not, as a rule, perform miracles to convert his opponent. The real miracle is the 'miracle of the teaching.' Śākyamuni's teaching is 'accompanied by proofs'; "it must not be accepted out of respect; on the contrary, it must be criticized, as gold is proved in the fire[1]."

Now, O monks, are you going to say: We respect the Master and out of respect for the Master, we believe this and that?—We will not say so.—Is not what you will say to be true, that exactly which you have by yourselves seen, known, apprehended?—Exactly so[2].

This point, as many another, has been very well illustrated by Oldenberg. Buddhas do not liberate their fellow creatures. A Buddha is only a preacher, and he teaches men how to liberate themselves. Disciples accept his preaching, not only because it comes from a man who is visibly a saint, a *vītarāga*, that is 'a man free from passion,' and who therefore, according to the

[1] *Nyāyabindupūrvapakṣa*, *Mdo hgrel*, CXI.

[2] *Majjhima*, I, p. 265.

Indian opinion, is likely to be omniscient (*sarvajña*)—but because his preaching proves accurate, because, as says Oldenberg, "aroused by his word, a personal knowledge arises in their mind[1]."

Pascal says the same thing and he points out the deep reason of the prestige of the great spiritual leaders:

> On trouve dans soi-même la vérité de ce qu'on entend, laquelle on ne savait pas qu'elle y fût, en sorte qu'on est porté à aimer celui qui nous le fait sentir.

Buddhists are introduced into the realm of truth by Faith; they possess truth only by Sight. They walk by sight and not by faith.

It may be remarked that the position of the Brahman philosopher towards the Veda—more exactly, towards the Vedānta, the Upaniṣads—is almost the same. No human being would have discovered the great axiom of the Upaniṣads of the identity of the Self with the universal Self; but the truth of this axiom, once by faith it has been admitted, is proved beyond doubt by personal intuition.

3. Sight must be followed by *bhāvanā*, that is cultivation, exercise, meditation, pondering again and again, impressing.

[1] *Buddha*, tr. A. Foucher[2], p. 321.

As far as we can see, Cultivation does not bring an increase of knowledge, a more accurate or more extended intelligence of unpleasantness, impurity, impermanence, unreality. But it confers a firmer knowledge which enables the ascetic to look always at things as they are, without being ever deceived by their apparent pleasantness, purity, permanence, reality.

To be accurate and technical, *darśana* destroys six of the ten passions or errors (*anuśaya*) and turns an 'ordinary' man (*pṛthagjana*) into a 'converted' man (*srotaāpanna*); *bhāvanā* destroys the four remaining *anuśayas* (*pratigha*, *rāga*, *māna*, *avidyā*) in so far as they are concerned with Kāmadhātu, and turns the *śrotaāpanna* first into a *sakṛdāgāmin* (by the destruction of the first six degrees of these *anuśayas*), then into an *anāgāmin* (by the destruction of the remaining three degrees); *bhāvanā* again destroys *rāga*, *māna* and *avidyā* which are concerned with the Rūpadhātu and the Ārūpyadhātu, and turns the *anāgāmin* into an Arhat. There is no *pratigha* above the Kāmadhātu.

One of the simplest and most important of the 'meditations' is the 'meditation on loathsomeness' (*aśubhabhāvanā*). We should like to describe it shortly, not to bring disgrace on Buddhism, but in order to give a more exact idea of the so-called 'spiritual training,' in order to portray more faithfully the physiognomy of the ascetic. There are in Buddhism so many lofty feelings, and also so modern an effort towards 'rationalism,' that the student—the compiler as well as the reader of a Manual—is likely to forget its Hindu features.

Visits to cemeteries, where unburied bodies are left to decay, are a duty of a monk, and there are in the Buddhist brotherhood ascetics who choose to live in cemeteries—the *śmāśānikas*, men of the cemeteries—in order to meditate uninterruptedly on the impermanence and the impurity of the body. The meditation takes on rather physical and emotional characters[1].

Ten 'cemeteries,' that is ten aspects of the dead body, are to be realized in turn,—to begin with the body one day dead, or two days or three days dead, swollen, black—to continue with an older corpse eaten by crows, with the corpse which has become 'this I know not what, something that has no name in any language,' but which the Buddhists are fond of describing at great length—to end with the bones rotting and crumbling into dust, as they have been washed by the rains of years.

The monk, for days and months, lives with the idea: "Verily, my body also has this nature, this destiny, and is not exempt."

[1] Warren, p. 360; *Yogāvacara Manual*, p. 53.

Such is one of the forms of the meditation on loathsomeness. When it has been practised long enough, it is not enough to say that the beauty and the form of a woman have lost their natural attractiveness: they are no longer perceived. The ascetic sees the skeleton only and the forthcoming putrefaction.

Despite its 'romantic' adjuncts, *bhāvanā* is an intellectual affair, the third degree of the realization of a truth.

To be taught impermanence, to be told that "Life ends in death" is one thing. Young men, 'infatuated by the pride of youth,' may agree to this statement: "Life ends in death," but they do not understand its true import. That is Faith, adhesion to the word of the Master. To ascertain this statement by personal inquiry, is what is called Sight. Finally, to ponder over it, until it becomes not only familiar, but actually always present to the mind, that is Cultivation.

IV

The path to deliverance would have been very reasonable—we mean, would be thoroughly intelligible to us—if the Buddhists had been satisfied with the realization of the Truths, positive statements to be believed, 'seen' or understood, 'cultivated' or pondered over; but the words Sight and Cultivation, explained as above, do not convey the true import of the Buddhist *darśana* and *bhāvanā*. A factor, a practically almost necessary factor of *darśana* and *bhāvanā*, is what is called concentration (*samādhi*), trance (*dhyāna*), attainment (*samāpatti*)—a non-intellectual element.

The history of trance is a long and obscure one. Trance has been traced in the semi-civilized civilisations. Just as penance is a common practice among the medicine-men, the sorcerers of old, even so trance is an archaic device. It was admitted that Man obtains, in semi-hypnotic states, a magical power. The name of a thing is supposed to be either the thing itself or a sort of double of the thing: to master, during trance, the name, is to master the thing.

Just as penance, trance became a means to spiritual aims.

That is the case with Brahmanism. Trance is the necessary path to the merging of the individual Self into the universal Self. To speak more accurately, there is only one Self, which is immanent in Man. For a time, the knowledge of our essential identity with this Self was looked upon as sufficient. But the actual feeling of identity was soon considered as necessary. Such feeling is impossible in ordinary consciousness; therefore it must be realized in trances, trances to be induced by hypnotic devices, the same as were practised by the sorcerers, protracted rigidity of body, fixity of look, mental repetition of strange sets of formulae, suppression of breath. Further, the immanence of the Self is a very materialistic one: it has its seat in the heart, where it is felt stirring and from which it directs the animal spirits; it makes its way along the arteries...Psycho-physical exercises are necessary to concentrate all the vital energies in the heart, that is to withdraw the Self from the not Self[1]. Hence the intricate discipline known as *Yoga*, with trance as an essential element.

It is only fair to state that the position of trance is, in Buddhism, a quite different one. Trance, like asceticism, is not an essential part of the Path, even if it were admitted that it is practically necessary, *d'une nécessité de moyen*, to use a phrase of the Catechism.

[1] Barth, *Religions of India*, p. 71.

Buddhism teaches in so many words that not every trance is good. A trance which is not aimed at the right end, eradication of desire, is a mundane (*laukika*) affair. When undertaken with desire, in order to obtain either advantages in this life, namely magical powers, or some special kind of rebirth, trances cannot confer any spiritual advantage. Of course, if they are correctly managed, they succeed, as any other human contrivance would succeed: a monk or any man who devotes himself to the concentration called 'of the realm of the infinity of space,' in order to live for centuries in the realm of the 'gods meditating on the infinity of space,' will be reborn in this realm, provided he has not to pay some old debts in hell or elsewhere; he will live there for centuries, as he hoped for; but he will die there some day and continue migrating.

But, on the other hand, it is an ascertained fact that Śākyamuni obtained 'enlightenment' by the practice of trances, and accordingly every monk has to practise trances if he is to make any progress. The more Buddhism discourages 'mundane' trance, the more it extols 'supramundane' (*lokottara*) trance, that is trance entered into, in order to cut off desire, by a monk who endeavours to get possession of the

Truths. The intention of the ascetic and his moral preparation make all the difference between mundane and supramundane trance.

Our texts clearly state that several of the Buddhist trances were practised by non-Buddhists, and scholars agree that the Buddhists did actually borrow from the common store of mystical devices.

The actual aim of trance seems to be, in Buddhism, twofold: to strengthen the mind, to empty the mind.

1. By means of trance, the ascetic concentrates the mind, strengthens the power of attention, gets rid of distraction. There are many technical contrivances, among which the ten *kṛtsnāyatanas* which seem to deserve special notice[1].

The monk makes a disk of light red clay—such as is found in the bed of the Ganges—one span four inches in diameter. He sits at a distance of two and a half cubits from the disk, on a seat of a height fixed by rule: if he were to sit further off, the disk would not appear plainly; if nearer, the imperfections of the disk would be visible; if too high, he would have to bend his neck to look; if too low, his knees would ache. Then the meditation begins: the ecstatic has to look at the disk as long as it is necessary in order to see

[1] See Warren, p. 293.

it with closed eyes, that is in order to create a mental image of the disk. To realize this aim, he must contemplate the disk sometimes with his eyes open, sometimes with his eyes shut, and thus for a hundred times, or for a thousand times, or even more, until the mental image is secured. All the time he conceives indifference for sensual pleasure; he reflects on the qualities of Buddha; he affirms his confidence in the efficacy of the exercise he is performing.

2. Trances may be defined as efforts towards an actual simplification or emptying of thought; as endeavours to get directly rid of the very ideas of I, mine, being, non-being[1]. As it is said:

When being and not being no longer stand before the mind, then thought is definitely appeased.

The method is not a view, either discursive or immediate, of impermanence or unsubstantiality, but a mechanical process.

The mind, once concentrated (*samāhita*) and strengthened by exercise with the clay disk or any other exercise of the same kind, is successively to abandon its contents and its categories. The ecstatic starts from a state of contemplation coupled with reasoning and reflection; he abandons desire, sin, distractions, discursiveness, joy, hedonic feeling; he goes beyond any notion of matter, of contact, of difference; through the

[1] See Mrs Rhys Davids, *Psychology* (1914), p. 110 foll.

meditation of void space, of knowledge without object, of nothingness, he passes into the stage where there is neither consciousness nor unconsciousness and finally he realizes the actual disappearance of feeling and notion.

It is a lull in the psychical life which coincides with perfect hypnosis.

At a moment which has been previously determined—modern physicians explain how this is possible—the ecstatic comes back, through the same successive steps, to the world of the living.

Does he come back in exactly the same condition as he was before? Can he practise these 'spiritual' attainments again and again, every afternoon after he has taken his only meal, sitting in an empty room or under the shadow of a tree, without being psychologically and corporeally affected?

The Buddhists believe that the mind remains, as it were, perfumed by the trances. For some hours or for seven days, sensation and cognition have been completely stopped. The ideas of I, mine, being, not-being are likely to present themselves again—as a matter of fact, they present themselves again as soon as mental life begins afresh—but they have lost their inherited power of arousing desire; they have been 'attenuated': "The mind of a monk who has risen from the trance of the cessation of feeling and notion is inclined to isolation, has a tendency to isolation, is impelled to isolation." Thus says Śākyamuni.

We willingly agree. The professional ecstatic is likely to forget how to see exterior objects: the mental reflexes he has cultivated turn to be more real than the changing appearances; in the same way, the ecstatic hears mysterious sounds. He becomes inaccessible to the desires that are born from the senses, inaccessible to pain, for his nervous sensibility is almost destroyed; he is happy; he is a Saint; he will not be reborn, because he has introduced into the series of his thoughts such a number of blank spaces that the further generation of thought and desire is stopped.

V

There are many aspects of Buddhism, which are more attractive than the aspect we have been studying. Apart from the religious developments known as Mahāyāna, older Buddhism owes the popularity which it has enjoyed in

India and which it enjoys in the West, not to its intricate theories on the soul or on the Path, but to its moral features, to the charming, if enigmatic, personality of the Master, to the mild wisdom of its gnomic poetry, to the legendary literature (Birth Stories) which contains so much folklore, humanity and wit. In fact, we have been busied with the most abstruse side of Buddhism, and, by no means, with the most important from the historical standpoint. But, from the philosophical standpoint, it is useful to make out clearly the reasons why this old query "Is Buddhism, since it is atheist, a religion?" is not a real problem. An inadequate knowledge of the nature of Indian mysticism and of the twofold nature of Buddhism is responsible for the confusion that is implied in such a view. Secondly, Buddhists have been credited with opinions concerning Soul and Nirvāṇa, which are by no means correct. I venture to think that it is worth while to consider anew these important and controverted points, and that, while the last word will never be said, our endeavours towards a more truly Buddhistic interpretation have not been utterly vain. My late friend Cecil Bendall willingly confessed that the only means to a right understanding of a religion is to believe in this religion. I am not prepared to say that I am a Buddhist, and moreover it is too late to take the *pabbajjā* under Sāriputta; but I have spared no pains to think and to feel as did the 'yellow-robed monks' who have rendered so eminent services, not to mankind as a whole, but to India, to China, to the Far East.

Nihilism 152

Oldenberg (H.) 13, 16, 75, 116, 142, 155
Oltramare (P.) 18
Omniscience 127, 156
Organs 39
Origination of cognition 39

Parents 61, 78
Patience 99
Penance 70, 142
Personality of reward 47
Pessimism 108, 121, 132
Philosophasters 61
Pischel (R.) 75, 123
Plato 43, 69
Poor and sick 78
Pragmatism 135
Prajāpati 21, 142
prāṇa 35
Premeditation 72
Preparation (of karman) 72
Principal action 72
Profound sleep 109
pudgalavāda 134
pūjā 3
punarmṛtyu 25
Punnā 9
P[illegible]ssapa 63
Purifications 70, 73
puruṣa 26, 37

Rationalism 32, 139
Receptacle world 101, 104
Re-death 25
Reincarnation 54, 84
Ripening of action 88
Rishi 71
rūpa 40, 71

Sacrifice 21, 22, 73
Saint 113, 153
Śakuntalā 102
Sāṃkhya 7, 37, 116
saṃkrama 48
saṃsāra 25
saṃtāna 51, 97
saṃvara 94
Śāriputra 9
sat 21
Śatakratu 73
satkāyadṛṣṭi 46
sattvaloka 101
Self-love 75
Series 51, 97
śīlavrataparāmarśa 74, 145
Similes:
  Chariot 41
  Child and girl 52
  Fire 69
  Fire in a jungle 53
  Flavour of salt 110
  Leaves of the Siṃśapā grove 127
  Lump of salt 89
  Milk and curds 51
  Physician 136
  Poisoned arrow 129
  Potter's wheel 28
  Seed dyed a certain colour 87
  Shoes 151
  Telephone 49
  Tigress 137
Sin 46, 69, 74, 83, 89
skandhas 35, 40, 44
Soma (Haoma) 19, 22, 23
Spinoza 5
Subtle body 35, 39
Sūfi 5
Suicide 147
Sun and Sungod 101
śūnyāgāra 152
Superstition 74
svabhāva 100
Svayambhū 21

Taine 38, 75
tapas 70, 142
Thomas (E. J.) 43, 106

tīrtha 7, 140
Totemism 18
Trance 160
Transfer of merit 33
Transitoriness 44
Transmigration 6
Truths, the four 152

ucchedadṛṣṭi 45, 51, 136
Unbelievers 60
Unintentional murderer 69
Upaniṣads 7, 63, 75, 140, 156
Upāsaka 74

Vāc 24
Varuṇa 13, 20
vāsanā 71
Vedānta 7, 37, 116, 125
Vedic gods 14
vibhavatṛṣṇā 131
Vinaya 148
visaṃyogaphala 88
Viśvakarman 21
vītarāga 155
Volition 68
Vows of religion 71

Warren (H. C.) 48
Whole and parts 42
Widows 59
Wrong view 46, 76

Yajña 3
Yājñavalkya 64
yakṣa 15
Yama 13, 46
yāna 4
Yoga 7

CAMBRIDGE: PRINTED BY J. B. PEACE, M.A., AT THE UNIVERSITY PRESS.

INDEX

Aborigines 16
adhipatiphala 100
Agni 21, 23
Agnosticism 126, 130, 133
ahiṃsā 17
Ajātaśatru 63
Ajita kesakambali 62
amṛta 9, 128
anāgāmin 91
Aṅgulimāla 90
Animism 35
Annihilation 45
antagrāhaparāmarśa 131
antarābhava 83
Āryans 11, 16
asat 21
aśubhabhāvanā 156
Asura 21
ātman 26
avijñapti 71

Back (of the action) 72
Barth (A.) 14, 15, 28, 37, 49, 50, 161
bhājanaloka 100
bhakti 3, 59
bhāvanā 156
bhavatṛṣṇā 131
bhikṣutā 74
Birth (projection of a) 92; birth-consciousness 54, 84, 97
Body 146
Boyer (A. M.) 24
Brahmā 104
Brahmā's palace 104
brahmacarya 141
brahman 27
Brahmans 18
Brahmans and *pravrajyā* 150
buddha 8
Buddhism as a religion 30
Butcher 71

Cemeteries 158; men of cemeteries 148, 158
Child and girl 52
Childers (R. C.) 123
Compassion 99
Confession 72
Continuity 50
Cosmogony 100
Cow, cult of the 17; vow of 147
Creation 104
Cultivation 156

Davids (T. W. Rhys and Mrs) 8, 9, 40, 44, 48, 49, 98, 104, 118, 147, 163
Dead, cult of 11
Death 83, 145
Debts, four, 150; leaving one's debts behind 91
Dependent origination 81
Desire and rebirth 64, 86
Destiny 63, 94
Devotee 74
dharma 3
dhūtaguṇa 148
Dialectic 124
Disciplines of salvation 1
Doer 95, 97
Duality 28
durgati 77, 108
Dying consciousness 86

Elements, four, 43, 62
Emaciated Buddha 143
Existence 51

Faith 153
Field (*kṣetra*) 78
Fire-sermon 146
Ford-makers 7, 140
Four-branched dilemma 111
Free will 96
Fruit of ripening, fruit similar to the action, fruit of mastery, 92, 100

gandharva 63, 85
Ganges 62, 70
Gift of *dharma* 99; gift of gold 68; merit of gift 77
Gods in Buddhism 101; Vedic 14
govrata 147
Gradual deliverance 123

Henotheism 19
Henry (V.) 22
Heredity 88
Hermits 148
Hopkins (E. W.) 59
Hypercosmical 7, 88, 162

Identity 50
Immediate sins 90
Immortality 9, 128
Individual 41, 134
Indo-Europeans 3, 11
Indra 21, 73
Insight 154
Intermediary existence 54, 85
Iranian gods 3
Īśvara 103

Jains 9, 67, 147
Jātakas 46
Jaṭilas 65
jina 98
jīva 26, 126
Jīvā 109
jīvanmukta 28, 119

Kāla 22
Kāma 22
Karman 57; migration of 49
kramamukti 123
kṛtsnāyatana 163
kuśala 76

Life 82
Loathsomeness (meditation on) 156
lokāyata 61
lokottara 7, 88, 162

Mahākāśyapa 147
Mahāyāna 6, 23, 123
Mallikā 75
Māluṅkyāputta 128
Māra 102
mārga 4
Materialists 61
Mātṛceṭa 111
Maudgalyāyana 9
Mental organ 39
Merit 72, 77, 78
Middle path 144
Migration of karman 49
Milinda 41, 146
Milk and curds 51
Milton 121
Mistakes, the four 152
mithyādṛṣṭi 46, 76
Momentaneity 44, 51
Moralism 100
Morality 73, 99
Müller (Max) 19, 124
Muni 142, 143
Murder 52, 71

Nāgasena 41, 146
nairātmya 34, 55
Nanda 79
nāstika 60

CPSIA information can be obtained at www.ICGtesting.com
Printed in the USA
LVOW11s0932140913

352445LV00019B/757/P

9 781177 690751